# Vengeance Is
# MINE

## A Story that Needs to Be Told

TO DIANE
OUR GOOD FRIEND
DANO.

# The Book of Dano

VENGEANCE IS MINE

ISBN: 978-1-77069-130-8

Printed in Canada.

# Contents

## Acknowledgements

First, I would like to thank my brother, Critter, for being the most solid person I have ever known in this life. Even though his life was taken from us by the reaper, he did not die in vain. I was meant to endure the experiences I've had from losing him, so that I could become the man God has planned for me to be. I understand this now, and I am very grateful to have received this wisdom from the Lord. I love you, my brother, with all my heart, and I look forward to spending eternity with you. God allowed Satan to have his weeds choke out my brother, but I realize that it was necessary so that I could be tempered in the refiner's fire. Without this conditioning, I would not be able to do the work the Lord has planned for me in this life. God has chosen me to convey his light to the world. Satan, the fight is already won and you lose!

Second, I would like to thank my mother, Rose, for being the rock she has always been throughout my life. She is truly a gift from God, and she has always stood fast in the ways of the Lord. Mother, you have always been good and hard on me when I've needed it. Without your guidance, I would have crashed and burned a long time ago. You have been a good example for your children in this life. You taught us that it's more important to give than to receive, and you have always given everything you've had to others. You surely have banked favour in heaven. I never had a father in this life, but I never needed one with a mother like you. God couldn't have given your children a better mother. Thank you for always being there Mom, whenever anyone has needed you. I will always love you.

Third, I would like to thank my brother, Mick, for believing in me when I had no faith in him. After all was said and done he told me, "Dano, I always knew that you'd make the right decisions for yourself in the end." Thanks, bro, for your love, support, and not judging me when I was going through my trials.

Next, I would like to thank my best friend, Bugz, my wife, for being there with me throughout the worst time of my life. We first went out two weeks after my brother was murdered, and neither of us knew what lay ahead for us. She's supported me without judgment for many years now and I thank God for her. I love you, Bugz. We beat him!

Finally, I would like to thank our Father, Yahweh, our Creator, for making me who I am. I love you, God, with all my heart, all my mind, and all my soul. Thank you for giving us our brother Jesus, and access to the fruit of the tree of life again. I know that we can't make it in this world on bread alone, so I will share the fruit you have given me. I will convey your light in this life, so that your wheat will flourish in the darkness of this world. I do not feel worthy of this task, but I will do what you have planned for me. I didn't understand at first why you picked me to do this for you, but I know that in your infinite wisdom you have your reasons. You have not given many men the light which you have given me, even though they wanted it. I am truly grateful for my soul's awakening. Thank you for not letting me burn in the refiner's fire. I am grateful to be able to lay down my life for my brother, for there is no greater thing. I will love my enemies as you command, and walk the walk as Jesus did. I will live as your example in this world. I have been saved by the power of your amazing grace. Hallowed be thy name, Yahweh.

Amen.

Part One

# Choked Out by the Weeds

# Chapter 1

# My Roots

I was born in a major city in the Pacific Northwest. I came into this world the only son of my mother Rose and my father Jack. Jack had a son named Will from a previous marriage. I never grew up with Will, because he was raised on the coast. The first time I met him I was seventeen. Before that, I didn't know he even existed. He was a hippie kid who never grew up. Both Will and Jack died of stomach cancer around the age of forty-five. In both their cases, their doctors found the cancer too late and just sewed them up on the operating table. They couldn't do anything.

My mother Rose had three children before me — two boys and one girl. Not even a year after I was born, my mother discovered that my father was cheating on her. She gave him only one chance. He chose to continue with his infidelity, so she left him. My mother then had one more son after me, and his name was Critter. Critter was three years younger than me and was my best friend growing up. He followed me everywhere, and we did everything together. My mother and his father split up when he was only a year old. My mother didn't have much luck with the men in her life, so she raised her children by herself from that point on. She was the best mother God could have given us. We didn't need a father with the quality of mother she was.

Jack had three more sons after my mother left him. He fathered them with the women he had committed adultery with. He never helped my mother financially to raise me. He never gave her one dime throughout my life.

I didn't meet him until I was seventeen. I remember going out for dinner with him and Will. He wanted to pay for my steak, and I told him, "That's okay. You've never paid for anything in my life so far! Why bother to start now?" Then I gave him twenty bucks for my meal and drinks.

I met my three younger brothers that same day. I have two families now. Jack died of stomach cancer a year later, and I only saw him the one time. I liked him, but I don't think I missed out on much by not having him around. Sometimes not having a father around is better than having one. Not one of my younger brothers he fathered knows God. I blame Jack and their mother for that. I pray that the Lord will come into their lives and change them. My hope is that they will wake up one day and know their Creator as I do.

The main male figure in my life growing up was my mother's older brother Rocky. He was a firefighter, and he retired from the service with the rank of assistant chief. My uncle was also a naval gunner during the Second World War. He served on a frigate in the Atlantic. When he was in high school, he was a boxer, and he won the golden gloves. He was a real man's man.

As a child, I attended the Church of the Nazarene until I was about thirteen. Both sets of my great-grandparents started to attend there in the early 1900s, which makes me a fourth generation Nazarene. As long as I can remember, I have known God. God has always been in me. Even if I tried to say that there is no God, it would be like saying there is no moon. It would be an outright lie. Sometimes you can't see the moon, and it appears like it is not there, but we all know that it's there. God is the same way, and the author of the poem "Footprints in the Sand" knows this. Sometimes when you are being tested in this life, it seems like God is not there, but I assure you that he is. There is only one set of footprints in the sand during these trials, because God is carrying you. Believe me, you are not walking alone. I have been there and I know firsthand. I am his living witness! I grew up without a father, but I didn't need one, because Yahweh is my Father in heaven.

I excelled in sports as a kid and I was an exceptional athlete. I played baseball in the summers, and hockey during the winters. The teams I played for won numerous city championships throughout the years. In school, I wrestled and played volleyball. I was very fortunate to have a really good coach. He had competed in wrestling during the 1968 Olympics and the Pan American Games. Our wrestling team did very well over the years. We won many team titles and championships. As a young boy, I was in Cub Scouts, but I quickly became bored with it. My uncle suggested naval cadets. I really enjoyed the cadets and immediately joined the guard. The cadets taught me how to shoot and sail. I became an excellent shot at a very early age. When I was sixteen, I started big game hunting and went out hunting every year with my uncle and my best friend, Ray.

Bruce Lee was one of my favourite characters when I was growing up. I really admired him for his fighting skills. I first started watching him on the Green Hornet television series during the early sixties. None of this Batman and Robin stuff for me. I didn't have any desire to watch Superman or any crime fighter wearing tights.

I also liked boxing. I watched Cassius Clay win the Olympics and followed him throughout his professional career as Muhammad Ali. I was a fighter at heart and a natural-born warrior. I always identified with characters like Daniel Boone and Robin Hood growing up — you know, the defenders of the weak who were not afraid to take on evil men. My favorite movies were action types, like Billy Jack and First Blood.

I was also fascinated with the ancient world as a kid. I really liked the story of David and Goliath. My interest in the old world arose naturally from the stories in the Old Testament. I have always been an Indiana Jones at heart. I loved to study Egyptology and learn about any civilization that had built pyramids.

I started to study the fighting art of Chinese boxing at a very young age. I wanted to learn Kung Fu like Bruce Lee. I was very fortunate to be able to train with one of the most highly skilled Chinese Kung Fu Masters. He was one of the first masters in North America to break tradition and teach white students. My Sifu grew up in mainland China and learned from his godfather the Southern Siu Lum styles. (Sifu is a Chinese word for teacher, or student of higher learning.) I studied Foo Hawk Pai, Lung Ying, and Buck Mei under him. I excelled in Chinese boxing, and used it to stay off the streets. I eventually reached the rank of Sifu myself. I earned a fourth-degree black sash and I am a master instructor.

I got into a lot of fights in my younger years and unfairly practiced my techniques on bullies. I was only 5'9" and a hundred fifty pounds until I was twenty-five years old, but I never took any crap from anybody. Nobody messed with me in my old neighbourhood growing up. Eventually, I grew up and matured. I started to feel very guilty about all the physical damage I had inflicted on others, even if they deserved it.

I dropped out of school and started working at a very early age. My mother wasn't impressed. One of my first jobs was working in a hospital in the morgue. After that, I received training as a transport operator and I operated heavy boom trucks. I enjoyed operating different types of heavy equipment, and I was good at it.

I returned to school after splitting up with my first wife at the age of twenty-five. Eighteen months later, I received an advanced high school diploma and started university. I studied secondary education. I majored in the biological sciences and physical education.

What I really wanted to do was be a firefighter like my uncle, but I was never afforded the opportunity professionally. The idea of saving lives and property while helping people really appealed to me. I feel that the firefighter's uniform is the only one truly worth respecting. My uncle taught me that there is no greater thing than laying down your life for your brother. He instilled in me that it took real courage to help people in the face of death. I admired him for being a war veteran and a firefighter. He was a real man to me. I really respected my uncle.

# Chapter 2

# Law Enforcement

When I had the chance to study law enforcement, I jumped at it. I graduated with honours in the police sciences. My passion was for crime scene investigation and forensics. I was trained by the police service's bomb unit. The training I received originates from the military, which makes it highly restricted information. I received training in IEDs, various types of charges and explosives, as well as different detonators, switches, and triggers. Upon graduation, I went into municipal policing and was put in charge of my own detachment.

While working with some officers from another police service, I witnessed several instances of corrupt policing and some serious violations of suspects' civil rights. I took it upon myself to initiate a joint service investigation into my fellow officers' criminal activities. Numerous charges were laid, and successful convictions were obtained for assault, drug possession, and fraud. One officer had his appointment removed and he can never work in law enforcement again. He was fined and put on probation. I feel that he should have done time for his crimes, but I'm not the judge.

I couldn't believe how I was treated from that point on by my fellow officers. I had crossed what is known as the thin blue line and they didn't trust me anymore. I felt they should have respected me for what I had done. Instead, I was a rat to them! What a bunch of hypocrites! Their mentality was no better than a bunch of convicts. I decided after this experience that there was no future in policing for me. I promptly resigned from my appointment. Oh well, that was law enforcement's loss.

While attending college and studying law enforcement, I met my second wife. She was studying elementary education and graduated with honours. She was eighth out of over eight hundred graduates that year. She was a very intelligent person academically, but I found out way too late that she had no real common sense life skills.

After I was finished with my experience in law enforcement, I worked as a Teamster. Around this time, I was involved in a very serious motor vehicle accident. I couldn't drive a truck anymore, so I had to find a new career. There were tough economic times in the early nineties, and I had a hard time finding work. I was lucky enough to get a start as an electrician. My income really suffered, though. I went from earning $29 an hour to a starting rate of only $8.50 an hour. For the next year, my finances were really strained. I was trying to support my old standard of living on less than one third of my previous income. I went further and further into debt trying to get retrained.

I didn't see what was coming next.

I came home from work early one Friday afternoon and caught my wife moving out. She said, "I need my space, and I need to be on my own for a while." She packed up what she wanted and left.

I couldn't keep our fourplex, so I moved into a small apartment in my old neighbourhood. I went to school and finished my first period of electrical training. I finally got a raise and started working again for the next couple of months. In April, I returned to school and started my second period of electrical training.

# Chapter 3

# Divorce

**M**y wife left me at the end of February, and by May I was very distraught. I loved her and hadn't seen this coming.

I sought out some professional guidance and help. One of my mother's best friends was one of the top psychologists in the city. I tried to contact him, but I found out he was quite ill. I discovered that his sister was also a clinical psychologist who practiced in the city, so I went to see her. I explained to her what had happened with my wife and told her how upset I was. She tried to tell me that there were far worse things that could happen in this world than having your wife run out on you. I had no idea just how right she was!

"You should just go see your wife and give her an ultimatum," she said. "She's had plenty enough time to make up her mind by now, and she should know exactly what she wants to do."

Our anniversary was coming up on May 23, and I didn't want to have any of our anniversaries spent apart if we were going to get back together. I invited her over for dinner so we could talk. "I'm not interested in reconciling, and I want a divorce," she said. Ironically, at this exact moment, a bottle of champagne that I had chilling in the freezer exploded! There was nothing I could do but accept her decision.

Marriage is like a game of chess. If one of the players decides not to play anymore and dumps the board over, that's it; the game's over. You can't pick up the pieces and start over, no matter how much you want to. It takes two players who want to play.

When I split up with my first wife, I put myself through three years of self-inflicted torture for nothing. I did this because I thought I really loved her. I realized later that I was more in love with her beauty than her brains. We only had one fight in the five years we were together. Her brother had ripped us off and the fight was over him making restitution for what he had done. It turned out that blood was thicker than right or wrong with her, but I wasn't raised that way. I'm really glad now that I stuck to my principles and let her go in the end. I learned a good lesson about self-inflicted grief. There was no way I was going to do that to myself again.

I had no idea that my wife was committing adultery. I found out later that she was out fooling around with a welder who had two of his own welding trucks. I guess she was just out for the money. She got pregnant from this guy while she was still married to me and had an illegitimate child. I heard she married him and he turned out to be a bigamist. When this guy married her, he already had a wife and two children. She's now raising his kid on her own.

Ironically, years later I was working at a power house, testing a motor. I needed an electrical outlet for the job at hand, so I approached a nearby welder and asked if I could use the receptacle on his welding machine for a power source.

"I'm going to be testing a motor in the building for the next week," I said.

"No problem," he said. "Since you asked me first, you can use it as long as you need to. Most people around here are ignorant, and they just do whatever they want."

As I stood up, he read my name on my hard hat.

"Do you know who I am?" he asked me.

"I don't think so. Did I work with you somewhere before?"

Then he asked if I had once been married to my ex-wife. At that moment, I realized who he was. I slapped him upside the shoulder! I said to him, "Thanks for asking me first before you used my wife!" I thought to myself, *You ignorant hypocrite!*

For the next week, he kept talking to me like I was his long-lost buddy. He was bragging to me about the beautiful little baby boy he'd had with my wife. As I was listening to him, I gave him no more recognition than water off a duck's back. It was a good thing it wasn't twenty years earlier, or I would have used him for sparring practice right there!

Then he told me how five of his buddies and himself had won the lottery. They'd won almost three million dollars and split it six ways. When my ex-wife found out that he had committed bigamy, she sued him for divorce, and she got the whole thing. He said, "The judge gave her my two welding trucks, and the house. I have nothing left, and this is why I'm out here working."

I laughed in his face! "Better your money than mine," I told him.

He kept carrying on about her being all about the money. I said, "Go away! What don't you get about this picture? I'm not your long-lost buddy. You had an illegitimate child with my wife, and you have the nerve to brag to me about it? Don't worry, I don't blame you for her infidelity! You couldn't have done her unless she let you! I've heard enough of your crap! Stay away from me from now on, whether it be on this job site or some other one in the future!"

When you come into that kind of money in this life, I see it as a test. I believe that my ex-wife will fail her test. She's a very insecure person. She only cares about shallow things like money and prestige. I know she will never use that money to help any other person in this world — you know, someone who could really use the help. She's too busy worrying about herself. It's too bad!

I forgive her for what she has done to me, and I leave her judgment to the Lord. I actually believe that she did me a great favour without knowing it. I didn't realize it then, but the relationship I had with my ex-wife doesn't hold a candle to my current marriage. I finally have the right wife now! Thanks to the Lord!

Chapter 4

# My Brother's Missing

It was a beautiful spring day in June. Just as I arrived home to my apartment, I received a phone call from my brother's friend, Rock. Rock asked me if I had talked to Critter lately. "Critter's not answering his pager," he said. "I've been trying to get a hold of your brother for over a week."

I explained to Rock that I had been very busy with my studies, and that I hadn't talked with Critter for a couple of weeks. "The last time I talked with my brother was on Friday of the May long weekend," I said. "We talked on the phone for a while, but I didn't see him."

The night after I last talked with my brother, I was woken out of a deep sleep. My name was called out loud by my grandmother. I recognized her voice immediately. I hadn't heard my grandmother's voice for over twenty years. She had passed away when I was sixteen. I hadn't personally experienced anything like that before, but my mother has many times. While grow-ing up, my mother would tell us when someone had called her name in her sleep, or if her ear would start ringing. Every time this happened, a close family member would die. The Irish call this a form of the banshee. I witnessed this many times through-out the years, but never experienced it for myself. I immediately told my mother about it, but I had no idea what it meant at the time.

After talking with Rock, I decided to try contacting my brother. I called his pager number, but I didn't get a response. I tried several more times over the next few days, but Critter still didn't get back to me.

Critter lived in our mother's basement suite, so I decided to call her. "When was the last time you saw Critter?" I asked.

"Saturday morning of the long weekend," she said.

"His friend Rock is concerned because Critter hasn't been answering his pager for over a week. I tried to call him myself, but he hasn't contacted me either. Something's not right, Mom! He should be answering his pager. This is really weird. I think Critter's missing! Mom, you should contact the police, and file a missing person's report. No one has seen him or heard from him for a couple of weeks."

She didn't seem to be too concerned, though, and down-played it. "You know how he likes to party," she said. "He sometimes takes trips to the mountains. He'll call or show up soon."

I had two tough weeks of finals left in my technical training, and I had to keep my head wrapped around my studies. While driving home one afternoon from school, I spotted my brother's truck parked a block south of the river valley's main drive. I circled around to check it out. I wanted to make sure it was Critter's truck.

It was parked in an erratic manner. The rear wheels were five feet from the curb and in the middle of the crosswalk. I knew right away that Critter would never park his truck like this. It looked like it had been parked in a real hurry. I went directly to my mother's house and got a spare set of keys for his truck. I went back and checked it out. It was Critter's truck all right, so I parked it correctly. I left a note inside his truck, asking him to contact us right away because we were worried about him. We didn't hear anything.

The next weekend, I returned to his truck with Rock and we moved his truck back to my apartment parking lot. I searched his truck for anything unusual, but I didn't find anything. The vehicle was just about out of gas, but everything else seemed to be in order. The note I left for him was still in the truck, and I found a receipt for some beer on the seat. It was dated Saturday, May 25. I took the receipt inside my apartment and put it away. Rock and I both knew something was amiss.

I called my mother again. "I'm getting really concerned, Mom. Tell me everything you can remember about the last day you saw him."

"He was going to Lung's to party for the weekend," Mom said. "I haven't talked to him since. I'll give Lung a call and find out when he last saw Critter."

Lung Phuc was a Vietnamese refugee Critter had been friends with since they were thirteen years old. Critter was now thirty-three. I guess they had known each other for about twenty years. His name, Lung, meant dragon. I guess he had lived up to his name. Satan is the dragon in the Bible, and Lung sure turned out to be a little devil. I called Lung "Miami Rice" because he thought he was pretty cool, and quite the big-time player. He was a really good kid when he first came to America with his older brother back in the early seventies. Lung grew up in Vietnam during the war. I can only imagine the terrible things he witnessed growing up there as a little kid. He had told us a few stories.

But Lung changed over the years. He was a really talented artist and could have made a good career at it, but he decided to be a drug dealer instead. He was slowly dragged deeper and deeper into the underworld. The easy money and excitement of his new life fooled him. He started out selling controlled drugs like Talwin and Ritalin on the drag, and then moved into the big-time, selling rock cocaine and crack. I told Critter to stop hanging out with him because he was bad news. Critter didn't judge him, though. He continued to be his friend and just turned a blind eye to his dealing.

I finally finished my second period of technical training and decided to put all my time into finding my brother before returning to work. My mother said, "Lung told me he hasn't seen Critter since Sunday, May 26. Critter told him he was going up north to work, and that he would be back in a couple of weeks."

This didn't make any sense to us, because Critter hadn't come back home. He didn't pick up his tools or work clothes. He couldn't go to work without them. It was now the fourth week of June, and no one had heard from my brother in over five weeks.

I decided to talk with Miami Rice myself, but he didn't trust me anymore because I used to be a cop. I got his phone number from my mother and called him up. The first thing he wanted to know was how I had gotten his phone number. "From Critter's phone book," I told him.

I discussed with him what he had told my mother. He told me pretty much the same story, except for a few more details.

"Critter went up north to work for a couple of weeks," he said.

"This doesn't make any sense," I pointed out. "Critter didn't take any of his tools or work clothes. He also would have told our mother where he was going. Critter hasn't answered his pager since the long weekend, and you were the last person to see him."

"I'll call around, okay? I'll check with some of our friends and see if anyone has seen him."

Lung didn't sound right. He was very nervous, and he was asking way too many questions. He was definitely fishing during our conversation. I've had a lot of experience with interrogation techniques, and my questioning skills are very well-developed. Something was definitely not right with Lung's story, and he was acting very uneasy.

Next, I went to my mother's house. We discussed everything Lung had told her. Then I told her what he had said to me. During our conversation, we discovered that he had told us two different stories. In fact, he changed his story several times. I found out that my mother had called Lung a second time. She said, "Lung changed his story from our first conservation to our second."

I asked her to call the police, because I knew something was definitely wrong. She still didn't want to. I insisted, but she wouldn't do it.

At this point, I decided to have a little face-to-face discussion with Miami Rice. I was going to get to the bottom of his story's discrepancies. The hair on the back of my neck was really standing up now! Something was really wrong! I knew in my gut that Lung was the common denominator. He knew a lot more than he was letting on. He was definitely hiding something. My sixth sense had never let me down, and it was tingling.

I called up Miami Rice and demanded a face-to-face meeting with him. He made every excuse in the book for why he couldn't meet with me. I explained to him that if I had to come and find him, it wasn't going to be a very healthy experience for him! He finally agreed to meet with me in the river valley in front of one of his apartment buildings. He had a lot of different places around the city that he used as stash houses.

When he showed up to meet me, he had his ol' lady with him. She was a prostitute who worked as a call girl for an escort service.

"Leave her here and get in my vehicle," I told him. He was very scared and apprehensive. She was really checking me out, and then she wrote down my license plate number. "If you have nothing to hide, you have nothing to worry about."

So he jumped in my vehicle and we left her there.

I drove across the river valley and parked exactly where I had found Critter's truck. I wanted to see his reaction to this location. He was extremely nervous, and he wasn't behaving in his usual Tony Montana tough-guy routine. Once we parked, I started to go over the discrepancies in his stories. He again started to change some of the facts. At this point, he was really getting nervous.

Then his ol' lady phoned him. I made the inference that she was phoning him to make sure he was alright.

I thought to myself, *You must be pretty worried, Lung, to have her call you and confirm you're alright.*

Then he started telling me about certain people who might have had a reason to hurt Critter. He was trying to direct suspicion on two other sets of people. He explained some possible scenarios to me. Lung was definitely trying to divert the suspicion from himself. He asked me not to let them know that it was him who had put me on to them. None of this made any sense. He was acting really erratically, almost like he was schizo. I thought he was doing too much of his own coke.

Next, he tried to convince me that we should go for a walk down into the river valley, to what he called Critter's favourite place. He said, "We might find Critter there." This really raised a flag with me. Why would he say something like this? Why would he think Critter would be there? Why did he want to get me down into the river valley bush? What was he trying to do? Set me up or kill me, most likely!

I grabbed him and searched him. I made sure he wasn't packing a gun or weapon of some kind. I made it clear to him that I wasn't going into the bush with him.

"What you are saying doesn't make any sense," I said. "Why would Critter be in the bush?" I took him back to where I'd picked him up, and left him there unharmed with his little girlfriend. They were both very scared.

After I dropped off Lung, I went directly to my mother's house. I told her everything that had just gone down with Lung. I explained to her how he had continued to change his story about what had happened on the last day he saw Critter. This

was the fourth version he had given us. I told her how he wanted me to go down into the bush with him and look for Critter
in what he referred to as Critter's favourite place. I was really
upset now! I knew something really bad had happened to my
brother. I knew it in my gut. Critter had been killed and this
little dirtbag knew all about it.

I had no idea why Lung would want to kill him, but he
definitely knew what had happened to my brother. I didn't believe Lung had the balls to kill my brother, but he could've had
someone else do it for some reason. I was really starting to get
upset. If my brother was dead, I wouldn't stop until I got every
frigging last one who'd had anything to do with it! I'd freaking
destroy them all! Those scumbags had messed with the wrong
guy's brother. I didn't know what to do next. I decided to go and
do some field intelligence on Miami Rice.

First, I contacted the couple which he had tried to put the
suspicion on. My brother had known this couple for years. Lung
had claimed that Critter went and partied with them after he
had last seen him.

"We haven't seen Critter in quite a while," they told me.
"We never saw him on the long weekend."

They were acting a little weird, but I thought they were just
a little freaked out when I showed up on their doorstep out of
the blue. I explained to them that Critter had not been seen for
over a month.

"Lung is trying to put suspicion on you two for his disappearance," I explained. "Let me know if you find out anything." They assured me they would.

Lung was also trying to put suspicion on my ex-brother-in-
law and his uncle. I didn't bother trying to contact them because

I knew Critter would never have had anything to do with them. They were a couple of real losers, aspiring independent biker types and hardcore convicts, but not killers.

Miami Rice left me a message to contact him. I called Lung.

"Why did you tell them what I said?" he asked. "I asked you not to tell them. I'm trying to help you, and you give me up. Now they won't trust me anymore."

I was just playing them against each other to see who was lying. Lung then asked me a really strange question. He wanted to know where Critter's ring was.

"What ring?" I asked.

"The one with Jesus on it," he said.

"I don't know. Why do you want to know where it is?"

"I really like it, and I'd like to buy it from you."

"I can't just sell you his ring, even if I knew where it was."

This was a really strange thing for Lung to ask me. I didn't understand what it meant at the time or its significance.

# Chapter 5

## One Solid Critter

I have seven brothers and one sister. My sister was the second oldest in my family. She really loved our youngest brother, Critter. His disappearance really stressed her out and it took a great toll on her health. Critter was the youngest of my three brothers on my mother's side. He was three years younger than me; the other two are older. I had four other brothers on my father's side; one was older and the other three are younger.

Ever since Critter started walking, he followed me around. He wanted to go everywhere I went. We were best friends growing up. He always had my back. I mean this literally. He would have followed me to the center of hell and back! If there was anyone in this life I would pick to have watching my back, it was him. I trusted him more than all of my other brothers put together. He was the most solid person I have ever known.

Critter had landed his first job when he was only ten years old, working as a theatre usher. One fall day, I went to watch a show at the theatre where he was working. He came up to me with a bloody nose and a tear in his eye.

"What happened?" I asked.

"I asked this kid to put his cigarette out in the theatre," he told me. "The kid refused to put it out, so I tried to kick him out of the theatre. He got up and punched me in the nose."

"Show me who did this to you," I said.

We walked into the theatre and he pointed the bully out to me. There were three of them sitting in a row beside each other. They were all at least two or three years older than me. I was about fourteen at the time.

I walked up quietly and sat down behind them. The kid that punched my brother had long hair and was sitting between the other two. I reached over the seat and grabbed him by the hair on the back of his head. I pulled his head back, looked at him straight in the face, and yelled, "Punch my little brother in the head?" Then I smacked him as hard as I could with a hammer fist right in the nose. His nose just exploded! There was blood everywhere and his nose immediately swelled up to three times its normal size. Then I threw his head back. I got up, walked back to the lobby, and sat down in a chair.

Next, the doors to the theatre swung open and one of his friends came running at me. I only had time to stand halfway, in a football ready position. I charged forward as he was coming at me and we collided. I pushed him back into the corner and started punching him in the nuts as fast and hard as I could. I must have punched him in the nuts ten times in two seconds. At the same time, my little brother was beating him in the head with his theatre flashlight. This was one of those big chrome types that the cops used to use in the sixties. It was about fourteen inches long with a four-inch head.

The other two guys just stood there watching, not wanting any part of us. Neither did the theatre owner, who fired my little brother right there on the spot. He didn't care about what had happened. He just didn't want any of his ushers beating his patrons in the head with flashlights. We all got kicked out of the theatre for life. I told you he had my back! He was only ten years old at the time and he displayed a lot of courage for a little kid. These guys were at least six or seven years older than him, and at least two feet taller. One thing none of the men in my family lack is courage.

Critter had a very good nature. He wasn't mean or violent in any way. All his life he had a special connection with animals and people. That's why I called him Critter. One summer when we were teenagers, we had this job painting an old cabin. There was an old tree with a squirrel in it. He would walk up to that tree and knock on it. Then he would ask the squirrel to come out, and it would. That squirrel would come right up to him and it would eat right out of his hand, but it wouldn't come near me. Critter loved animals and was always bringing home strays. He brought home our cat when it was just a kitten and we had that cat for about eighteen years. His name was Tom and he was a pretty cool cat. In fact, Garfield reminds me of our old cat.

When Critter was a kid, he saw a movie about a hobo who signed his name everywhere he went. This hobo signed his name, "Kilroy was here." Critter started to do the same thing from a very early age. One year while traveling with his friends, he put his name everywhere from coast to coast.

Critter knew so many people. Everywhere he went, he ran into somebody he knew. He had a lot of friends all over the country who thought the world of him. Whenever I was traveling throughout the years, I was simply amazed at how many places I had seen his name written. I still see it everywhere I go around the city, and this is over forty years later.

Critter was always helping people, and he would stop anything he was doing to help someone. One winter, he froze his hands really bad helping an old couple get their car unstuck in the snow. It was about thirty below late one night when he came across them. He was driving along without any gloves, but he got right out of his car and helped them anyway. He didn't feel how bad the cold was and he suffered severe frostbite. Critter almost lost some of his fingers helping those people that night. He was very lucky and only lost a couple layers of skin.

"What were you thinking?" I asked him.

"Oh well, I didn't feel the cold," he said. He missed quite a few weeks of work healing from that good deed.

Critter was very protective of our older sister. She was married to a real winner who used to abuse her. Her husband, Manson, used to get drunk and then he'd become very abusive.

Critter heard one day that her husband had assaulted her, so he went over to see them. When he got there, Manson was drunk and getting smart. Manson was about eight years older than Critter. Critter was only about twenty at the time, but he was a pretty big boy. Critter grabbed Manson's bottle of whiskey and rammed it down his throat. He held it there until it was empty and then he pulled it out of his mouth.

"So you think you're pretty smart, slapping my sister around?" he said. "Well, let's see how smart you are now!"

My sister lived on the second story of an old house. My brother hung her husband out the second story window by his ankles. Manson was yelling and screaming for his life! Critter threatened to drop him if he ever laid a hand on her again. He didn't touch our sister again for many years. Finally, one day he pushed her down so she left him. I think she thought leaving her husband was a far better idea than Critter visiting him again.

My brother never had much use for the police. They constantly harassed him and his friends while they were growing up. Their harassment was completely unfounded. They were just implementing old school coercive policing, which is completely unacceptable today.

One night we went into our favourite local pizza joint. We had been hanging out in this pizza place for years. There was a table full of cops sitting there and I didn't recognize any of them except for Sergeant P.J. He was the only cop Critter ever respected. This cop was the only one who ever treated him and his friends decently.

Critter recognized the other cops. They were a bunch of new rookies who'd been bugging him a while back. Critter got up, went over, and sat down with them. He said, "Hey P.J., did you know there's a couple of goofs in here who think they're owls? You know, they think they're pretty smart."

The rookies said, "Who? Who?"

Critter and P.J. smiled at each other, then Critter got up and came back to our table. The rookies didn't get it at first, until P.J. spelled it out for them. The looks they gave us after that were priceless. To this day, I'll never forget it.

Critter served in the naval reserve. He was a good seaman and enjoyed the Navy's manoeuvres. He was stationed on a frigate and every summer they would go on missions up and down the Pacific coast.

One year, they were in Portland and most of the crew were on leave. There was a young, eighteen-year-old kid guarding the ship's gangway. This old sea dog of a petty officer was coming back aboard the ship drunk and was giving the kid a rough time. You're supposed to ask permission to come aboard the ship before attempting to, so the kid stopped the chief because he hadn't asked permission first. The old sea dog was bugging the kid because he had served on the ship for years and this was the kid's first mission. He said, "Who do you think you are, sonny boy? This is my ship and you should know who I am. What... do you think you can stop me from coming aboard my own ship?"

My brother was up on the bridge witnessing all this. He took the sub-lieutenant's hat and jacket out of the bridge and put them on. He went down to the gangway and tied into this petty officer really good! It was like something out of an Eddy Murphy movie. The kid was just freaking out the whole time because he knew my brother was not an officer. The chief just stood there and took it all. Then he kissed my brother's butt so that he wouldn't be charged. Critter threatened to have him arrested and thrown in the brig for being drunk and disorderly. Then Critter told him to get out of his sight until he was sober. The chief petty officer disappeared to his quarters. Then Critter went and put back the lieutenant's uniform.

About three days later, the chief finally ran into Critter face to face. That's when he realized Critter wasn't a lieutenant at all. The chief took Critter off to the side and told him, "If I didn't respect how much balls it took for you to do what you did, you'd

be the one in the brig right now for impersonating an officer."
Critter and the chief had a good laugh after that, and then they
became good friends. The kid respected Critter for what he had
done, and always looked up to him. It's a good thing the real
sub-lieutenant never caught wind of this story.

I told Critter many times to stop hanging around with Lung,
but he wouldn't listen to me. "Lung's bad news," I said. "He's
going to get you into trouble with his dealing."

Critter was like Jesus—he didn't judge someone by their
faults. Instead, he valued them for their good qualities. When
Jesus was associating with the known sinners and tax collectors
the company he was keeping was in question with the Pharisees.
Jesus responded to their accusations by saying, *"Healthy people
don't need a doctor, but sick people do. I didn't come to invite good
people to be my followers. I came to invite sinners"* (Mark 2:17, CEV).
Critter had the same attitude as Jesus. He had known Lung for
twenty years, long before Lung had joined the underworld and
started selling drugs. Lung had been a pretty good kid most of
his life, but still I told Critter to quit associating with him. He
wouldn't listen to me, though, and continued to be his friend.

The things I say in this life usually come true. Critter knew
this and had witnessed it several times throughout the years.
Whenever I would caution him about something, he would say,
"Why did you have to open your mouth? You know it's just
going to happen now." When it would happen, I would say, "I
told you so." Critter really didn't like me saying that. This time,
though, I hoped I was dead wrong! I hated to say it, but in the
back of my mind, I thought I was dead right! I really hoped he'd
turn up somewhere laughing at how concerned we'd all been. I
really didn't think it was going to happen, though. I hoped that

nothing bad had happened to my little brother. I loved him so much. I hated to think of what it was going to do to our mother if it turned out Lung had done something to him.

## Chapter 6

## Critter's Been Murdered!

I was driving over to Rock's when I received a message to call my mother. I stopped at a payphone and called her.

"I heard on the news that the remains of a man's body have been found in the river valley. The description of his clothing matches what Critter was wearing the last time I saw him, and they are looking for help from the public in identifying the remains."

She finally called the police and reported Critter missing. She told them, "Critter hasn't been seen since the May long weekend. It's been five weeks now."

Mom then called the medical examiner's office. They described to her the clothing the body had been found in, and it matched what Critter was wearing.

"The body has been there for quite a few weeks," the investigator told her. "The remains were recovered at 1800 hours on

Sunday, June 30."

She told me, "The body is at the medical examiner's office undergoing an autopsy. The body has no head or hands, which has made the identification of the remains more difficult."

"I'll be right over," I told her.

I hung up the phone and got back in my vehicle. I freaked! I just knew in my gut that it was my brother! I screamed at the top of my lungs, "No! God! No!" The connection was immediate—I now knew why Lung had wanted me to go into the bush with him!

When I arrived at my mother's house, I immediately called the homicide detectives, and they came right over. I explained to them in detail the chain of events which had taken place over the last five weeks. I told them about my meeting with Lung. I explained how he had wanted me to go down into the river valley bush with him to look for Critter. I told the police that I believed he wanted to get me down into the bush to do something to me. I never dreamed that my brother's body would be found in the bush. I explained to them that he knew where my brother's body was before it was discovered because he had told me this on Monday, July 1. The news release did not come out until the next day, on Tuesday, July 2. They confirmed that Critter's remains had been discovered on Sunday, but no news was released until Tuesday.

I suddenly realized that my dead grandmother had called out my name on the same day my brother was killed. I had experienced the banshee, just like my mother had so many times before.

They wanted to impound Critter's truck and go over it with their forensics unit. I took them to my apartment and released his truck to them. They let me know that a different detective was going to be assigned to the case. I met the new detective a couple of days later.

I phoned my brother Will to let him know that Critter had been murdered. To my astonishment, he said, "I know, I heard they found him." I couldn't believe it! How did he already know? Nobody in the family had told him. Nobody knew yet! Will continued, "I heard it through the grapevine."

"Who told you and what did they say?" I asked him.

He wouldn't tell me, so I hung up the phone on him! I hated to think badly of Will, but he was a cocaine addict and he was protecting his doper friends. Will had inherited hundreds of thousands of dollars from his great-uncle and grandmother, but the money had spoiled him and he became a useless junky. He lived in a small city five hundred miles west of us. He worked and partied with a guy named Blacky, who used to live here. Blacky's ex-wife was one of the people Lung had tried to cast suspicion on. I made the inference that this was the grapevine Will was referring to, but they couldn't have known anything yet either! Unless they were involved, or Lung told them.

Detective Given was the new homicide detective assigned to the case. When I met with him, we discussed how Lung had changed his story four different times. Given really pissed me off, by stating that it was just a matter of semantics.

"What do you mean, it's just a matter of semantics?" I asked him. "This guy knew exactly where my brother's body was before it was released in the news."

Given told me that I didn't have any proof.

"What do you call this?" I asked. "I'm a former police service member and a fully trained cop. Lung stated this directly to me. That's not hearsay!"

"It doesn't matter," Given said.

"Fine," I said. "I'll get you your proof."

Then I told Given about my conversation with my brother Will. I said to him, "Will already knew that Critter's remains had been found, and he told me that he'd already heard about it through the grapevine." I explained to Given that Will would not tell me who had told him about Critter. "I think Will's work partner, Blacky, is the connection. Blacky shouldn't have known anything yet either. The only way he could have known something is through his ex-wife! His ex-wife knows my brother and Lung."

"I'll contact your brother, and question him," Given told me. "And I'll talk with Blacky's ex-wife."

I called Miami Rice and tried to set up another meeting. When I phoned him, he didn't want to meet with me again. He said, "I don't know anything else and I can't help you anymore."

He came right out and told me, "I'm afraid of you! I know you think I killed your brother."

"Why would you think that, Lung?" I said. "Come and meet with me at my mother's house. She wants to talk with you, too. She has some questions to ask you about the last time you saw Critter. You owe her at least this, especially after knowing Critter for so many years."

My mother's house was a safe neutral place for Lung to meet with us.

I told him, "After all, Lung, my mother's husband is a retired police officer." So he agreed to come.

"A man's body has been found in the river valley, and maybe it's Critter's," Lung told me.

"How do you know this?"

"I saw it on the news."

"We have already talked with the police and the remains they found do not match Critter's."

He wasn't listening to me, though. He kept saying, "It could be Critter's." He was acting like he knew it was Critter's body for sure.

Before Lung arrived, I set up a video camera in order to record our conversation. He sat in my mother's house and bragged about all his cars, his possessions, and the properties which he had acquired with his drug money. I let him carry on so that he would start to feel comfortable. He was really acting like the big-time gangster he thought he was.

Then I discussed with him what we had talked about previously in my vehicle. I confirmed how he had wanted me to go down into the river valley bush with him and look for Critter. I also restated how we'd had this meeting on Monday, July 1, and he confirmed it. I also got him to admit how he had changed his story four different times about what had happened on the last day he saw Critter. I now had the proof I needed for Given! Lung didn't even have a clue he was being recorded. Man, I wanted to take him out right then and there, but I knew I couldn't. Patience, man!

I called Detective Given and asked him exactly where my brother's body had been discovered. He told me where it was found, and then I went down to the crime scene. I found the exact location where they had retrieved the body. Upon further investigation, I realized that they hadn't done a very good job. The scene had not been handled properly at all. I literally found some of my brother's bones, which they had missed. You have no idea what went through my mind at that exact moment! I had just dug up some of my murdered brother's bones out of the dirt! This was bone of my bone! Man, was I frigging mad! This really freaking pissed me off! I was so mad at the medical examiner's office!

I went to them, and requested to review their investigation file. They told me I had to get permission from my mother, who was the next of kin. She granted permission, so I was able to review the file. She wanted to see it for herself, so I had to talk her out of looking at it with me. Upon reviewing the file, I saw all the photos that had been taken at the crime scene. It was definitely my brother! His remains laid there without a head or hands. This was something no one should have to see! His body was pretty badly decomposed after five and a half weeks in the heat and rain. From the position of his arms, I knew he had been carried there and dumped. I knew it was my brother just from looking at the hiking boots and coveralls he was wearing. These pictures were pretty gross, to say the least. It was a good thing my mother didn't witness these graphic photos. They would have haunted her to this day. If I hadn't had the right training from my previous law enforcement experience, and my days in the morgue, these photos definitely would have caused me psychological problems.

I really tore into the medical examiner's investigator for doing such a poor job at the scene. I explained how I had dug up some of my brother's bones, which they had missed. He defended the job they had done. He explained to me how hot it had been on the day when they were out there. "We had to work into the night because we didn't get the call until after 1800 hours," he told me.

"I'm not impressed with the homicide unit," I said, "or the way in which they are carrying out their investigation." I explained to him that I was now conducting my own investigation.

"At least someone is finally making an effort," he responded.

I made the inference that he wasn't impressed with homicide's efforts either.

I set up a meeting with Detective Given, so that he could listen to the tape. I went down to the main police station and met with him in the homicide unit. He told me, "I questioned your brother Will, and he wasn't very cooperative! I don't understand why."

Given had asked Will, "Why don't you care about what happened to your brother?"

"He's not my brother," Will had answered. "He's my brother's brother."

I explained to Given that they were not actually brothers. Will and I had the same father but different mothers. Critter and I had the same mother but different fathers. Will didn't give a crap about Critter. It was more important to him not to rat on his drug addict friends. Some brother. Oh well, to hell with him!

Next, I played the evidence tape for Given. While I was playing the tape, he fell asleep. I couldn't believe it. Right there in front of me, he fell asleep while listening to the tape. I freaked! I woke him up and asked, "Why are you sleeping?"

He denied sleeping, saying, "I just had my eyes closed because it helps me concentrate on listening to the tape better."

"You're full of crap!" I said. "You didn't answer me until I physically woke you up. You had better start taking this seriously, man. My brother's been murdered!"

I was extremely pissed with this guy, but I knew that his main case involved a little girl who had been abducted, murdered, and then raped. He'd been working on her case all night. Still, that was no excuse for him falling asleep while listening to the tape. I got him the evidence he needed, and he was still acting apathetic. Screw you, man!

I got up and told him right there, in front of all of the homicide cops, "Lung might be walking around breathing, but he's a dead man! I'm telling you he's as dead as dead gets! You mark my words! My God is not the money god, and Lung's going to pay for what he's done! He thinks he's gotten away with killing my brother! Well, it's not going to happen!"

They were all right there, ready to arrest me for uttering threats, but they couldn't because I had only stated a fact. I didn't make a threat. Then I walked out of their office and said, "How's that for semantics, Given?"

That was it. I was done with these cops. I didn't have much faith in the criminal justice system to begin with, and that's why I had left the service in the first place. I was going to take care of Lung myself. To hell with them all. It seemed like none of these cops really gave a crap about what had happened to my brother. I believed they were treating my brother's homicide apathetically because of his history with them. That's okay, because they were going to find out that there was at least one person on this planet who did give a crap—me. Detective Given should have arrested Lung immediately after I gave him the tape. I had absolutely no idea why he hadn't yet.

I started to hunt for Lung again. I looked for him everywhere for a couple of months. He must have gone into deep hiding. I couldn't find him anywhere.

I finally crossed paths with him accidentally. I started to follow him while he was doing his drug deliveries. I almost took him out right there when he came out of his last drop, but I controlled myself. I continued to follow him.

I did field surveillance on him for a couple of weeks. He took me right to all his stash houses. I recorded all of the different vehicles he was using, and discovered his main connection. Through my observations I was able to locate their gang's warehouses, including the main one where all their dealers were operating out of.

I started to realize I was getting too worked up! I needed to step back from this thing. I didn't want to make any mistakes and wind up doing something irrational out of anger. I really frigging hated this guy! Never in my life had the thought of doing somebody in entered my mind, but man I wanted my pound of flesh! He was as dead as dead got, man! What a waste of breath!

## Chapter 7

## He Moves Mountains!

I decided to go to La Puente and visit an old friend of mine. While I was there, I went to a party with my friend's son. At the party, I met a Cholo, an ex-Chicano gangbanger whose brother had been murdered the year before. We had a good talk at the party. He told me, "God has enlightened me not to seek revenge for my brother's murder. The Lord made me realize that it had to stop with me, or my mother would lose her only other son." That was a good resolution for him, but it wasn't my situation at all.

Overall, it was a good trip. I cooled down like I needed to while I was there. When I got back home, I remembered what Jesus taught us, if you have the faith of a mustard seed you can move mountains. Moses knew this and he parted the Red Sea with God's power. So, I talked to God. I asked him with all my heart, all my mind, and all my soul, "Please God handle this in some other way! If you don't, you know what I'm prepared to do! I don't want to, but I will if I have to!"

It was the first week of December and I started to look for Miami Rice again. He was nowhere to be found. It was like he had left the planet. Right around this time, I got a phone call from a mutual friend of Critter's and Lung's. She told me, "Lung's in the hospital dying of bone cancer."

I couldn't believe it. I called the cancer hospital and they confirmed it. They told me that he was no longer in their care because there was nothing else they could do for him. He had been transferred to the palliative care ward of another hospital.

I rushed up to the hospital to see him. I wanted to gloat at the circumstance he found himself in. When I arrived at the hospital, I saw his brother there visiting with him. I wanted to see him alone, so I left. I came back the next day, but his lawyer Harley was there. I recognized Harley right away. I guess he was helping Lung put his affairs in order. Lung was currently charged with some pretty serious drug charges. His lawyer represented some pretty heavy criminals, like big-time drug dealers, bikers, and dirty cops. He was quite good at his job. He seemed to win most of his cases, or at least he made good deals for his clients. Lung told him, "This is the brother of the guy that we were talking about." Harley left immediately! I found it odd that Lung immediately told him who I was. Why had he done this, and why had Harley taken off so fast?

I finally got my chance to see Lung alone, and he was quite surprised to see me. The first thing Lung asked me was, "How did you know I was in here?"

"It doesn't matter," I said.

"My bones are so sore!" he told me. "It feels like someone is sticking red hot coat hangers in them."

"That's really too bad! I really feel for you, man! You know, Lung, you have no idea how lucky you are to be in here!"

"What?" he replied with a serious look of shock on his face.

"I wanted to go on a little trip with you west of the forestry trunk road," I said. "I wanted to give you the opportunity to come clean, so that you could tell me exactly what happened to my brother! Don't worry, though, Lung. I would have left you breathing with a bucket of bear bait on your head!"

"I only have six weeks to live at most," Lung said. "I was talking with my parents in Vietnam. My mother's a Catholic now and she wants me to get a priest, but my father has always been a Buddhist and he wants me to get a monk. I don't know which way to go."

I never would've believed what happened next unless I lived it! I did a one hundred and eighty degree turn. He wasn't playing his tough guy role anymore. He knew he was going to meet his Maker real soon, and he was just a scared little boy. You know, the person who's really inside us all, the one that's left after you tear down all the secular malarkey we all create to present ourselves to the world.

Instead of gloating like I had planned to, I took pity on Lung. I explained to him how to save his soul. "The only way to the Father is through the Son." I explained John 3:16 to him and how he had to pray to God in order to seek forgiveness from the Lord. I told him, "You have to acknowledge Christ, and why he died for you. Jesus shed his blood on the cross in order to wash our sins away. This is the only way you can be forgiven for your sins. No priest, or monk, can do this for you! You have to do this for yourself, and mean it! This is the only true way to eternal life, and heaven. No matter what you have done in this world, Lung, it's never too late to wake up and truly repent." I let him know that God's eternal grace was the best gift he could ever receive, and that no man could hide what was really in his heart from God.

He looked at me and broke down. He started crying and said, "I'm really sorry for getting your brother killed." He was sorry for living his life the way he had. "If I only had another chance to live, I would never live my life this way."

He still wouldn't tell me who killed my brother, though, or exactly why it had happened. He was afraid for the safety of his brother and girlfriend once he was dead.

I left him to die and never saw him again. I don't know whether he ever prayed to God to save his soul or not. I couldn't believe what I had just done for the man who was responsible for my brother's murder. I had gone into the hospital wanting to gloat at him. The last thing I thought I would ever do is tell him how to save his soul. You don't know who you really are until the time comes… then you find out. Wow, I couldn't believe it. This sure was a far cry from going on that trip with him. The Lord truly does work in mysterious ways.

That night, I went to my mother's house and told her what had happened at the hospital. Then I called Detective Given at the homicide unit and told him as well. I said, "I told you Lung was dead, he just didn't know it yet! I told you, my God is not the money god!"

Given had told me months before, "I don't believe in God because of all the terrible things I have witnessed on the job. There can't be a God! If there is, how could he let these terrible things happen?" Then I heard the detective say to his fellow officers, "You'll never guess who's on the phone. It's Dano, and he says Lung's in the hospital dying of bone cancer."

The next day, Given went up to the hospital and questioned Lung. Lung denied telling me that he was sorry for getting my brother killed. Given came over to my mother's house after he left the hospital.

"Lung told us some pretty disturbing things which you said to him at the hospital," Given said.

"Oh well, it really doesn't matter now, does it?" I asked him to drop the drug charges against Lung, so that he could go home to Vietnam and die with his family. The prosecutor's office did drop the charges and Lung went home to Vietnam with his girlfriend. He died near the end of January.

Now we would never know who had actually killed my brother, or why. The truth was buried with Miami Rice. Thank you, my God, for hearing me when I cried out to you and for taking care of this in some other way! You literally moved this mountain for me. I love you with all my heart, all my mind, and all my soul! I will never forget that you did this for me!

It finally came to me why Lung was asking about Critter's ring. He must have been there when they murdered my brother, and he must have looked for Critter's ring before they dumped his body. Critter wasn't wearing his ring when they killed him. Lung had to have known this, and that's why he was asking about Critter's ring. When I put my brother's bones in his urn, I put his ring in it with them.

I never had anything to do with Will after the way he acted towards Detective Given. I was really mad at him for refusing to tell the police what he knew. As far as I was concerned, he was dead. He wasn't my brother anymore. He later ended up contracting stomach cancer and died like Lung. Was this just situational irony, or was this his destiny, too?

I went to see him one last time before he died. I wanted to ensure that he understood John 3:16. We went out for dinner, and I discussed it with him. He assured me that he knew what it was all about. "I was going to pay for our last meal together," I told him, "but I've decided not to because you're still an addict. I'm not going to free up funds for you so that you can have another fix!"

I never went to his funeral. I forgive him now. I know that the drugs he was using destroyed his proper thinking. They destroy so much in this world.

The woman who was the grapevine connection between Lung and Will was the same person Lung had tried to cast suspicion on—Blacky's ex-wife. The last time I had talked with her was when she told me about his bone cancer. She'd asked me if she could have something of Critter's to remember him by. Critter had this art print of a thief in the night, so I made a copy of it and hung it on her front door. She freaked out and took it as a threat. She phoned Given and cried to him. He questioned me about it.

"She asked me for something of my brother's," I told him. "It's no big deal. I just honoured her last request."

"It's a pretty scary picture," he said.

Jesus instructed us not to be caught off-guard in this life because he will come like a thief in the night. Maybe her guilty conscience was making her paranoid.

"It's not my issue," I told Given. "I gave it to her intentionally to see what kind of reaction I would get it. I guess I got one."

One night, I heard a noise upstairs, so I went up to check it out. I thought someone had invaded the house. As I approached the living room, I went to turn on the light switch, but it wouldn't work. I rapidly turned it on and off several times, but the lights wouldn't come on. At this moment, I noticed a large dog in the living room and it looked like a white wolf. It was just sitting there by the chair looking at me. Then I heard a laugh coming from the other side of the room — it was Critter. He just looked at me laughing while I tried frantically to turn the lights on!

Then I woke up from my sleep and realized I was dreaming. Man, was this dream real! I believe that every dream has a message, if we can only understand its meaning. I thought about this one for a while. I believe my brother was trying to let me know that he was okay. Critter was using symbolism to communicate with me. He was letting me know that I would never be able to turn his lights back on, and by laughing he was showing me that he was okay on the other side.

Part Two

# The Refiner's Fire

# Chapter 8

## A New Can of Worms

A few months had passed since Lung died of bone cancer when some new information came to light about my brother's murder. First, a friend of my brother's came forward and told me everything he knew about the people who had murdered him. He showed me the location of the shop they were dealing out of. Next, I talked with an informant from the coast who I didn't know from Adam. She told me how they had killed my brother, and she also described in detail the vehicles that were used when they disposed of his body.

"A very powerful lawyer is the head of this organization of criminals, and they are very dangerous men," she said. "If they ever find out that I helped you, I'm dead. This lawyer lives in a red brick mansion in the city, and he comes from old money. One of their gang members is a mole in the city police service." She was adamant that I never disclose to anyone who she was,

because she didn't want to be murdered, too! These informants didn't know each other and they were two completely independent sources of information.

"He's a white male of Eastern European ethnicity, and he's
a very big man," she said, describing the mole. "He's quite tall,
about 6'3" or more, and he is well-built, like a bodybuilder." She
didn't know his name, but she knew he was a sergeant with the
city police service. "He has a history of abusive arrests, and the
head of their gang defended him on these charges. He's around
forty years old, give or take a couple of years."

I can't disclose much more at this point without jeopardiz-
ing the evidence which could be used in future prosecutions.
The only way either of them would share their information with
me was if I promised never to reveal who they were. Apparently
my brother indirectly found out the identity of this mole in the
police service. His so-called friend Miami Rice then let this gang
know about it. This officer had been on the inside of the police
service for over twenty years. Evidently, they had murdered my
brother to protect their mole's identity and send a message to
the rest of their organization.

The female informant made me promise not to ever give up
her identity to anyone. She knew that as long as this mole was
active on the inside of the police service nobody could be trusted. I had no idea, at this time, how dirty the police service really
was. These people were serious criminals and would stop at
nothing to protect their interests. She told me some very specific
details about this dirty cop and the man who was head of this
gang. I decided to share this information with the homicide unit,
and give them one last chance.

I called up Detective Given and met with him and another detective at a downtown coffee shop. When I met them there, I noticed some federal homicide cops there as well. I recognized them from my days in the service, and I asked Given, "Why are they here?"

"It's just a coincidence," he told me.

I didn't buy it for a second. They were checking me out. Something was definitely up, but I didn't know what. I explained to Given that two informants had shared with me some very important information about my brother's murder. He wanted me to tell him who they were, so that he could talk with them.

"I gave them my word that I wouldn't tell anyone who they were," I said. Then I explained to him who had killed my brother and how they did it.

I told Given that the female informant had disclosed to me some very specific details about this dirty cop, but she didn't know who he was. I also told Given that she knew exactly who the head of this gang was. He was a very good defense attorney who had been practicing criminal law in the city for a long time. When she told me who he was, I made the connection immediately. It was Harley, and he was the same guy I had seen at the hospital with Lung. He was Lung's lawyer, and he was the head of this gang. He was a highly intelligent lawyer who usually won his cases. He only defended the big-time criminals and dirty cops. He had built a profitable practice defending his own.

After I shared this information, Detective Given said, "How are we supposed to find out who this officer is?"

Then the gang unit detective said, "Dano, we have fifteen hundred members on our force."

"It can't be that tough," I said. "How many forty-something 6'3" white sergeants do you have on the force who are built like bodybuilders and have a history of abusive arrests? Do your frigging job!"

I had just opened another can of worms with these guys. Every time I gave this detective some information, he came back with a negative response instead of running with it. I didn't understand him or what his issue was. Unless a tip was one hundred percent certain and spoon-fed to him, he had issues with it. I didn't know if he was useless or just ignorant. To tell you the truth, at this point I really didn't give a crap anymore! The meeting was done, and I was out of there!

I called up my oldest friend, Sergeant Moon. He had been with the police service for over ten years. I told Moon every-thing the informants had told me just in case something hap-pened to me. I knew that he was a clean cop, and he was the only one I could really trust on the force.

"The force knows all about Harley, and we've been trying to bust him for many years," Moon told me. "We've never been able to get anything on him, though. We've searched his man-sion and office numerous times without success. Harley is al-ways ready for us. It's like he's being tipped off. It makes a lot of sense to know there is a mole in the picture."

"I'm conducting my own investigation now," I told Moon. "I'll keep you informed of anything I find out."

## Chapter 9

# Field Intelligence

All I did for the next seven weeks was conduct field surveillance on these suspects. Everything the informants had told me about them was one hundred percent on the money! I recorded numerous hours of video surveillance on these scumbags and their activities. I found the vehicles that the informant had told me they used when they had disposed of my brother's body. She had given me a dealer's license plate number and it matched the tag on one of these vehicles. The numbers on the tag were 666. I guess they really did deal for the devil! One of their other vehicles had the same numbers on its tag as well. They must have special ordered their plates intentionally. They used dealer plates because it was easier to switch vehicles with them.

The more I observed these dirtbags, the more I wanted their heads. I was really going to enjoy this payback, but I could guarantee they wouldn't! I found out where all their businesses were, their homes, and their stash houses. They had quite an elaborate network. These people were very well-organized and had a lot of money. They didn't have a clue that I was on to them, though. They just went about their criminal activities because I was completely invisible to them. I couldn't believe the number of phony businesses they had. They were very active over this seven-week period, pushing their poison.

Next, I approached two of my family members for some support. I didn't expect them to physically assist me, but I could have used some moral support and financial back-up. I was ready to act. The police were totally useless in their efforts.

When I talked with my Uncle Rocky, I realized immediately that he wasn't the man I thought he was. Now that he was put to the test, he turned out to be all talk and no action! I had always looked up to him, and I respected him as the main role model in my life. He was a highly decorated World War II veteran. I respected people with courage. I had always tried to be like him, to be a real man — the secular model of a real man. You know, when the going gets tough, the tough get going. I had no idea just how ignorant I was. My Uncle Rocky had instilled in me from a very early age that there was no greater thing in this life than to lay down your life for your brother. I was prepared to do exactly that. Now he shied away and acted like it wasn't his problem. I guess he was too old and comfortable now, and had too much to lose. He got going all right — in the other direction.

Then I approached my oldest brother, Mick. He had been a clone of our uncle all his life. He'd served as an officer in the militia when he was a young man. He also studied karate when he was in school. I went to his house to tell him everything I had found out. He was having a nice little barbecue with his kid's schoolteacher. They were sitting around the table in his backyard.

"Let's go for a walk," I said. "I need to talk with you!"

As we were walking, I told him, "I just finished seven weeks of intelligence on these scumbags, and I'm ready to act." I explained to him that the only piece of their organization I hadn't figured out yet was the identity of the dirty cop.

He immediately distanced himself from me. "You're really sick, man, and you need some serious help." He directed me to stay away from him and his family. He really never gave a crap about Critter when he was alive, but Critter always loved him. They were fourteen years apart. I don't know why I had thought he would back me now. Maybe it was because we were brothers. I guess he had too much to lose now that he had his comfortable little life, but he wasn't finished living yet! Over the last several years, he'd been very nuclear. He really only cared about his wife and kids. He reminded me of my ex-wife; they were both very insecure. He'd lived his entire life worrying about what other people thought and how he looked. It was all about appearance with him.

Now I was really pissed off, but it was okay. I wasn't sick, but I sure was mad! Mad as hell! I was as mad as you could get! I cautioned my brother before leaving. I told him, "I'm going to hit these scumbags hard, with everything I've got; and I'm not going to be responsible for what could happen to you or your family." After all, Critter shared the same last name as Mick, and Mick's address was listed in the phonebook. "If you're going to take any precautionary measures, you'd better do it quickly! Because these people will definitely retaliate!"

With my training, I was fully capable of taking care of these scumbags myself. I really didn't need any help from him, or my uncle! After all, I was the most capable person I knew. I was just looking for some moral back-up.

*Goodbye, brother,* I thought to myself. *Thanks for nothing!*

Next, I went over to my mother's house. I told her how disgusted I was with my uncle and brother. They always talked about what they would do if someone ever hurt a member of their families. What a couple of mouthpieces they'd turned out to be! My mother told me that I didn't have the right to act on my own, and I argued with her.

"God has seen what happened to Critter and he will handle it," she said.

"As long as I'm alive, these dirtbags are not going to get away with killing my brother," I told her. "The criminal justice system has failed us, but I'm not going to!"

She knew how worked up I was and pleaded with me not to do anything. "What if they harm Mick and his family?"

"So what? He doesn't give a crap about what happened to Critter, so why should I give a crap about what might happen to him? He's lucky I even warned him!"

Then the phone rang. I received a phone call from my brother's cousin on the coast. He was a homicide detective out there. He started sticking his face in my business.

"Your brother asked me to call you because he's very concerned," he said.

"Mind your own frigging business!" I told him. "I'm not interested in your opinion or my brother's. Tell my so-called brother to suck it up and quit crying on your shoulder. Don't waste your time. It's a dead issue, and I mean dead!"

I knew what Mick was up to. He didn't want to rat on me for what I was about to do, but he was really scared. I knew he thought that I wouldn't act if he brought in an outside source, especially if it was a homicide cop, his little cousin. Man, were you wrong, Mick!

After the call, Mom told me, "I've been going through some of Critter's things, and I think you should have a look at them." She had found some phone numbers in a bowl beside his bedroom phone. As I was looking at them, I realized that one of them was a police pager number. I recognized it immediately, because I had called the homicide detectives so many times over the last year.

I asked myself, *Why did Critter have a cop's phone number in a bowl beside his bedroom phone?* Critter had never had anything to do with cops. He never liked cops since he was a teenager, and he sure didn't like it when I went into law enforcement. He used to say things to me like, "Run along and play with your badge," or "You go save the world and book 'em, Dano." He learned not to trust the police from an early age. They used to jack Critter and his friends up all the time in our old neighbourhood. They slapped them around more than once. After knowing the cops beat him up as a kid, it's not hard to understand why he had no use for them.

Then it came to me right away. This had to be the mole's pager number!

# Chapter 10

# Cornered the Mole

Icontacted Given right away and met with him. I showed him the phone number. I told him, "I'm positive this is the mole's pager number."

He downplayed it again, as usual. "This is a national pager number," he said. "Not only cops use this service. It could be anyone's, like a doctor's."

"Check out the number and see who it belongs to," I said.

Later on, he got back to me. "I couldn't find any police records for it at that time."

"If you don't investigate this pager number properly, I'll just call up this cop myself!" I said. "I'll arrange a meeting with him on my own, and I don't think you'll be pleased with the outcome of the meeting!"

I guess I put the fear of Dano into him. The next time he got back to me, he confirmed that it was a member's pager number.

He said, "I couldn't confirm how long this officer has had this pager number."

"Who is this officer, and what's his rank?" I asked. He confirmed that this officer was a white male sergeant. "I want you to arrange a meeting with him." Given didn't want to set it up. "If you don't arrange this meeting, I'll do it myself, my way!"

Then he said, "I've known this officer for years, and I highly doubt he could be the mole." As soon as I heard Given say that, I realized that he was biased and that he wasn't being objective. From that point on, I really started to distrust him!

I told Given that we had to be smart about how we handled the meeting. "We have to ask our questions very tactfully, and trap him." I said.

Given then interviewed the sergeant by himself. He asked him if he knew Critter by name, and the sergeant said, "No." Then Given showed him a picture of Critter and asked if he had ever met him. Again, this sergeant denied knowing him. He also denied ever meeting Critter. Given then asked the sergeant how long he had been in possession of his current pager number.

"It used to be my private pager, and now the police service is paying for it," the sergeant said. It turned out that the pager number had been in his possession long before Critter's murder.

Given then arranged a meeting between me and this sergeant. My mother demanded to be at the meeting with us. Given, my mother, and I met with him in his office at the station. He came in with Given and introduced himself, all calm and friendly.

"How can I help you people?" he asked us.

I responded by asking, "Can I see your police identification?"

He freaked! "Why do you need to see it?" he asked. "I am who I say I am. Detective Given knows me, and you're sitting in my office."

"Listen," I said. "Why are you so apprehensive to show me your identification? Doesn't the solicitor general give it to you so that you can present it to the public upon their demand?"

He got very agitated. He left the room, then returned with it. Upon examining his identification, I realized his last name was Eastern European — Ratkopitt.

He was a tall man, at least 6'3", with dark hair. He was very well-built, like a bodybuilder. I then confirmed the answers he had given to Given. "Do you know anyone named Harley?" I asked.

"No."

"Have you ever been charged, as a member of the police service, with using excessive force during an arrest?"

He started getting very upset. "What's this all about? And what does that have to do with anything?"

"Just answer the question, please!"

He then admitted to having been charged with assault many years ago. The charges had stemmed from an arrest he made.

"Who represented you on these charges?" I asked. He admitted that Harley was his lawyer. "I thought you didn't know anyone by that name." I'd just caught him in a lie, right there! As I looked right at Detective Given, I thought, *I knew it was you, you frigging dirtbag!*

He really lost it then. "Who do you think you are, trying to interrogate me in my own office?"

"You are not behaving properly. Not like someone who has nothing to hide. You've been a member of the force for over twenty years, and being a sergeant you should be more than happy to answer any of my questions. After all, I'm trying to get to the bottom of my brother's homicide. You know, Detective Given has been observing your behaviour all this time."

Then he settled down immediately and tried to control his demeanour. He knew I had just made him. He was behaving like the cornered rat he was. This mole was really digging a hole for himself. No pun intended. He wasn't used to being on the other end of an interrogation, and he was definitely blowing it!

"Can you explain why my brother would have your pager number in a bowl beside his bed?" I finally asked him. "Especially since you've never even met my brother! My brother doesn't have any use for cops, especially dirty ones!"

He didn't have an answer. I had him cold, and he knew it! It was nice to see him squirm like the little puta he was! What a big, bad, tough cop!

After the meeting, Given told us, "You still don't have any proof that Ratkopitt is the mole. Everything you have confirmed is just circumstantial."

"What the hell Given! What's your freaking problem? I told you ten specific details about this dirty cop months ago! He fits everyone of them to a T! What's the statistical odds of that, man?" I told him. "Ah, it really doesn't matter anymore anyway, does it? My mother and I know we've cornered this rat in his own hole. Whatever, Given! What's this sergeant's position with the police service?"

"He's a search master," Given said. A search master is in charge of collecting intelligence on missing people, and people suspected of being murdered. What a convenient position for this dirtbag cop! I discussed with Given the way Ratkopitt had acted during the meeting. It was obviously not normal behaviour, especially for a police officer with nothing to hide. Even if they never nailed him for being the mole, his days were numbered with the service. He couldn't be circumstantially linked to a murder investigation or a gang of organized criminals and keep his position. It would be too great of a security risk for the police service. I'm sure he had become a member of special interest to them from that point on. His career was finished!

While in his office, I had noticed some interesting pictures on the wall. Some of the people in these pictures were part of this gang of organized criminals! I told Given about the pictures, and I asked him to check them out.

## Chapter 11

## A Life for a Life!

This whole can of worms had been completely opened up again. I had thought this chapter of death was done in my life. I believed that all the knowledge of my brother's murder had been lost when Lung took his last breath. Man, was I wrong! I had no idea what was coming in the next few months. Now I knew the truth, and I was going to deal with it!

I have always known God, and he has always been in me. I love God with all my heart, all my mind, and all my soul. He is my strength. He's the voice inside all of us—your conscience, your gut feeling, your sixth sense. I stopped going to church when I was about thirteen. When I was twenty-five, I read the first five books of the Old Testament, as well as the first four books of the New Testament, but I was confused. I found the scriptures to be very contradictory! In the book of Genesis, God made it very clear that we are not to hunt down murderers and kill them! In other words, God said, *Vengeance is mine!* Later, he gave Moses the law. Then God said, *"An eye for an eye, a tooth for a tooth, and a life for a life."* But when Jesus came he made it very clear that we must be greater than the evil men of this world when he instructed us to turn the other cheek. But he also said, *"I didn't come to change the law."* Which is it? How can it be both?

These people had gotten away with murdering my brother. The secular justice system had failed us, and all I wanted was my pound of flesh. I wanted these dirtbags to pay for what they had done to my brother. I definitely didn't want them running around free, continuing to pump their poison into society. They were getting rich and more powerful all the time. I couldn't let them continue killing and wrecking people's lives. Evil only wins when a good man fails to do something, right? The Billy Jack's of this world know right where I'm coming from! They know exactly what I'm talking about. Someone had to stop them, and I was just the one who could give them what they deserved.

When I was a cop, I struggled with the thought of having to kill someone in the line of duty. Who gave the peacekeepers this right? Not God! God hasn't spoken to them and given them this right. The peacekeepers are appointed by people, and people have given them this power. But remember, we all answer to God. I decided back then that I would not shoot to kill. If I had to shoot a criminal, I'd shoot 'em in the leg instead. Fear of the Lord is the beginning of wisdom!

I needed some educated answers before I could act. In the back of my mind, I needed to know for sure that I was in the right. After all, my soul was on the line. This was not some stupid martial arts movie based on a vengeance theme. This was real life, and my actions would have eternal consequences.

I decided to go see the pastor of the church I grew up in, and get the answers I needed.

I walked into the church and introduced myself to the pastor. I closed his office door and told him, "What you are about to hear can never leave your office!" I made him give his word that it wouldn't. I explained all the facts of my brother's murder to him. I told him, "The criminal justice system has failed us and these scumbags have gotten away with killing my brother." I asked him point-blank, "Do I have the right to take out these evil men who murdered my brother? You know, *'A life for a life'* according to God's law."

To my astonishment, he didn't know. I sat in his office looking at his degrees on the wall. He had a degree in theology, and another one in religious studies. He was a very well-educated man in the scriptures. He had obtained a master's degree. He was a reverend in the church, but still he didn't know! I remember thinking to myself, *What good are your degrees if you can't even answer this basic question for me?* He sat there and continued to give me a bunch of secular reasons why I shouldn't do it. Like, I might get killed, or I might get caught and go to jail. I didn't want to hear that worldly crap.

As far as I was concerned, this pastor had failed me, so I left.

Oh well, he was only a man. I realized that I was looking for my answers in the wrong place. I needed scriptural proof. I said to myself, *You're a well-educated man. You're a college graduate. You've attended university. You know how to pick up a textbook and study it critically. You don't need anyone to spoon-feed you the answers. Go and find them for yourself.*

Over the next week, I studied the Bible and searched with all my heart, all my mind, and all my soul. I remembered what

Jesus had said — "*Ask, and you will receive. Search, and you will find. Knock, and the door will be opened for you*" (Matthew 7:7, CEV). So I started pounding at the door.

I thought to myself, *I'm not a Jew, so I'm not looking for my answers in the Old Testament.* I went straight to the beginning of the New Testament and started studying the four gospels.

As I was reading the gospels, each of them became a piece to the puzzle. They were like the transparencies which teachers use on overhead projectors in school. Each one contained a piece of the big picture. As I read each book, it was like laying another transparency on top of the last. After I read the fourth book, the picture was complete.

These books were written by four different men. Each of these men described the life of Jesus from his own point of view. They recorded his life and his teachings from their own perspectives. After I finished reading the gospels, I was changed forever. It was like I was looking at a three-dimensional poster, and I finally got the focus right. The image jumped right out at me. I was finally able to see the hidden image clearly. When I read the parable of the weeds, I received my answer directly from the Lord! Right then and there, my focus had been adjusted, and it was clear. His message jumped right out at me and it was immediately in my mind. I opened the door to him when I was twenty-five, and he kept his word. He did not leave me. My brother Jesus was there for me in my darkest hour!

The parable goes like this. A field owner planted a crop of good wheat, and while he slept his enemy scattered bad seeds in his field. As his crop started to form the heads of grain, his field workers noticed all the weeds. They asked the owner, "Where did all the weeds come from? You planted good seed in your field."

The owner said, "It was my enemy who did this."

"Should we pull up the weeds?" the field workers asked him.

"No, because you might mistakenly pull up some of the wheat along with the weeds. Wait until the harvest, and let the wheat and the weeds grow together. Then I will let the harvest workers pull up the weeds and burn them, and they will store all the wheat in my barn."

As soon as I read this, I had my answer. Thank you, my Father in heaven for my brother Jesus! He has shown me the way! I knew you wouldn't let me down, as men have. I had searched with all my heart, all my mind, and all my soul. God knew this, so he opened the door for me. What Bible had the pastor studied to earn his degrees? I found the answer I was searching for in the first day of studying.

Jesus spoke in parables because if you were meant to see the light, you would understand them right away, and if you were not, you wouldn't. In other words, if your cup is already full, you cannot add any more to it. If it is already full, you can look and look, but you will never see. You won't be able to see the forest because the trees are in the way. The only way you can receive the Lord's wisdom is with the mind of a child. You must empty your mind of what you think you know, and let it be like a sponge, not a rock. A child's mind is like a sponge. It is young and it absorbs everything immediately. It is not full of the world's secular garbage yet. It has not been brainwashed by society's malarkey and norms. You must not let your mind become a stone. A stone is hard, not porous, and it can never absorb anything. An old dog's brain is like a stone, which is why it can't learn new tricks. Hopefully you can be more than an old dog, but some people can't.

This is what the parable means. God is the field owner, and his field is the world. The good seeds of wheat are the people in this world who try to live their lives the way God wants them to. The weeds are the people who belong to the devil, and they live their lives their own way. The field workers are those who spend their lives working for the Lord, and the harvest workers are angels. God's angels definitely know the difference between the weeds and the wheat. The weeds will be pulled up and burned. The field owner's barn is the kingdom of heaven, and that is where the wheat and the field workers will spend eternity with Jesus. Amen.

Once I read this, I felt true humiliation for the first time in my life. My soul was stripped completely naked before the Lord! All of my steadfast convictions had been destroyed in a single moment! Everything I believed in meant absolutely nothing to me anymore. My way of thinking was totally changed forever. I was no longer the man I had strived to be all my life. I finally knew who I really was, and there was no turning back. I was in total shock, but I liked it. It was like a heavy load had been taken off my shoulders. I love you, God. You have restored my dignity through this humility. Thank you for my brother Jesus. I am finally secure in the ways of the Lord.

Then I started to think of the terrible mistakes I could have made. If I had acted, I could have pulled up some wheat mistakenly. What if one of the guys in this criminal organization was an undercover cop? I mean a real cop doing his job. Not a frigging dirty rat! I was prepared to take them all out, even the ones who were not directly involved with my brother's murder. After all, they were just a bunch of scumbags. Then I remembered some of my criminology education, how some people weren't given a fair chance from the start. These people were probably victims of their environment. Can you imagine if you were raised the son of a mafia member, or an outlaw biker? What chance would you have in this world of being a decent person? Just imagine growing up in that kind of an environment with that kind of conditioning. The only education you would receive in this world would be pure evil. You would be completely ignorant and not even know it. Look at how blind I was from this world's Christian hypocrisy and secular brainwashing, and I didn't even know it. How much worse would it be for them, being raised in their environment?

Make no mistake! Vengeance is a very effective and powerful tool of the devil! You cannot take justice into your own hands, because then it is no longer justice. This is what I call the Billy Jack syndrome. Do not be misled by it! I had absolutely no conscious awareness of how influenced I'd become from this subliminal form of conditioning. It's a good thing I had God in me. I've always tried to listen to my sixth sense. He raised this flag in the back of my mind. Some people might call this your conscience or inner voice. Thanks to God, I searched for the answers before I acted, and he opened the door for me!

After receiving the light, I decided to go back and see the pastor. I went into his office and told him what I had done. I explained how God had given me the answer I was seeking. "I now know that I do not have the right to weed his field," I said. "I now realize that these evil men could wake up one day. They could turn to the Lord and truly repent. No matter what evil they have committed in their lives, it's never too late for them to truly change. If I took them out, I would be taking this opportunity away from them. It's clear to me now that I do not have this right, because I am a man, a field worker, not an angel! I am not one of God's harvest workers."

The pastor's chin hit the floor. "Never have I seen the Lord work like this in a man's life!" He said, "You really have received the Lord's wisdom." The Bible says that there will be no greater celebration in heaven than when the worst of men truly wakes up, when they really change and turn to the Lord! Repent, you evil men! It's never too late!

The Bible also says that you should pray for the souls of evil men who have done you wrong, so that they will change and turn to the Lord. If they do not change before they die, your prayers will be like putting hot coals on their heads when they are in the fire. Do not make these prayers with the hopes of punishing them. Instead pray that they will truly wake up and be saved. We want to win souls over, not destroy them. That's Satan's job! Remember, God knows what is truly in the hearts and minds of men, and that is how you will be judged. I pray that Lung found his way to God through Jesus before he died.

# Chapter 12

# A Second Chance

After the Lord woke me up, I decided to turn the intelligence I had collected over to the homicide unit. I took in an edited copy of the video footage I had shot while observing these scumbags. Given wasn't interested in it, but he hooked me up with two detectives from the gang unit. After watching it, one of them said, "I can't believe our guys have been watching them for over a year and we have nothing this good. We need to use this as an example of how to conduct our video surveillance in the field from now on."

About two days later, over thirty businesses and homes were hit by police taskforces. Numerous arrests and seizures were made. The police really hit them hard, and right where it hurt them most. It cost them a lot of big money, and their freedom. Police seized drugs, money, and property. It was one of the most successful busts the service has ever had. Some of these criminals wound up doing major time, but lots of them made deals.

None of them were ever charged with anything connected with my brother's homicide. I'm resolved to the fact that the police will never charge anyone with Critter's murder. These criminals have gotten away with killing my brother. The only way the police service will ever nail them is if they rat each other out for some reason! It's okay; they are still accountable to God, and I completely trust in him. They haven't taken their last breath yet! The sky will fall one day!

Jesus said, *"When an evil spirit leaves a person, it travels through the desert, looking for a place to rest. But when the demon doesn't find a place, it says, 'I will go back to the home I left.' When it gets there and finds the place empty, clean, and fixed up, it goes off and finds seven other evil spirits even worse than itself. They all come and make their home there, and the person ends up in worse shape than before. That's how it will be with you evil people of today"* (Matthew 12:43–45, CEV). Well, this was exactly what Satan did to me, and I didn't even realize it.

Being the weak Christian I was, I kept dwelling on the fact that these criminals had gotten away with murdering my brother. I really didn't get any satisfaction from the fact that they took these major hits from the police taskforce. That didn't have anything to do with the murder of my brother. I kept slipping and thinking how much I still wanted my pound of flesh! I wanted some justice here and now. I wasn't thinking about how God had promised to take care of them in his own way.

The devil was working hard against me, and he really wanted my soul. I had no idea what was really going on. I kept feeling really guilty for not just taking these scumbags out. I knew that if I had been the one killed, my brother Critter would have just took them out without any second thoughts. Guilt, whether founded or not, is a very effective tool of the devil. Satan is always trying to mess with us psychologically. He's always trying to make me feel like I let my brother down by standing fast and listening to the Lord. These thoughts keep coming back into my mind over and over. My brother doesn't mean more to me than the Lord, but that doesn't mean I love my brother any less. Forget it, Satan!

I approached Detective Given with an idea. I told him, "I believe the police will never arrest these dirtbags for my brother's murder." I explained to him that the only way they would ever get these killers was if they ratted on each other for some reason. I wasn't prepared to wait for this. I made an offer to wear a wire, and be human bait. "I'm willing to go right up to the main enforcers of this gang, the ones who killed my brother, and provoke them to their faces. I'll let them know exactly who I am, and I'll call them out! I'm willing to do this on their own turf, where they feel safe."

These killers would never stand for this right to their face. "They will try to take me out right there!" I continued. "When they act, your tactical unit can sweep in and arrest all of them for attempted murder." Given didn't want to go for it because it was too dangerous. "Why not? I'm willing to put my life on the line. If they happen to actually kill me before your boys can arrest them, so what? Then you will definitely have them cold for murder. I'm willing to sign a release giving the police total immunity from any responsibility or criminal negligence."

He still wouldn't go for it. To hell with the police, and their secular enforcement.

I was really choked with the city police service. They were so useless. They couldn't do anything unless it was given to them on a silver platter — no pun intended, Detective.

I decided to go and talk with the federal police service. I told them how my brother had been murdered, by whom and their motive for doing it. I gave them the breakdown of this organization of criminals, and who the head of this gang was. I explained to them that this gang had had a mole in the city police service for over twenty years, and who he was. They were very interested. Then I gave them all the intelligence I had gathered to date.

They initiated an investigation of the city police service. Eventually their findings proved a connection between this organization of criminals and the city police. They were able to prove an ongoing association between some city police service members and members of this gang, but no criminal charges were laid. The police chief had to resign, and the service now had a national reputation for being a dirty police force.

The officers who were proven to be connected to this gang should have lost their appointments, but they didn't. The service brought in a new code of conduct for their members instead. From then on, the force's members could lose their appointments if they were caught associating with known criminals. At least something happened and the public became aware of how dirty the city police service really was.

I really had to get away now. I needed a timeout, so I went out to the country to visit a friend of mine. While driving back home on the highway, I was talking to God. I was apologizing to him for being weak. "I'm sorry for falling down. I know better, because you have already shown me the light. I'm really sorry for still wanting my revenge!" At that exact moment, I was just about killed!

I was driving on an undivided highway behind two tractor trailer units. I was following them for about ten minutes on a very curvy section of the road. A pickup truck was very close to me, riding right on my tail the whole time. Once the road straightened out, I started to pass the trucks. The pickup truck stayed right on my tail as I was passing, and then it passed me. Just at that moment, an unmarked police cruiser was going the other way and turned on its lights. It did a U-turn and chased us. I kept watching the cruiser in my mirror. I didn't know if this cop was going to stop me or the pickup truck that had passed me in front of him. We were both speeding. I was doing about twenty over the limit, but the pickup was doing about fifty over.

Just as I looked ahead again, the pickup was about fifty yards in front of me. At that exact moment, a semi was coming the other way towards us. The pickup crossed the center line, and hit the semi straight on. Talk about a real live IMAX moment! The semi kept coming straight at me! I thought I was dead for sure! I hit my brakes hard, but they kept disengaging because of the automatic braking system. I finally stopped five feet shy of where the semi crossed the road in front of me. That was the longest three seconds of my life! The semi continued on down into the ditch through a barbed-wire fence and into a farmer's field. I couldn't believe it didn't jackknife.

The cop drove right past me and stopped on the other side of the pickup to block traffic. I yelled at the officer, "What do you want me to do?"

"Help the trucker," he yelled back. I looked over at the truck, and there was nothing left from the driver's front side to the passenger's rear end. The truck was torn in two diagonally, and the saddle tanks were destroyed. There was fuel everywhere and the unit was just smoking. I thought to myself, *Do you really want to risk your life? This truck could explode at any time! To hell with it!*

I ran over to help the trucker. I couldn't open his door because it was buckled. He was out cold, and then he came to. We both worked on the door and got it open. I helped him down to the ground, but he didn't want to move anymore. His leg was broken from the firewall having crushed it, and his ribs were broken from impacting the steering wheel.

"My neck is injured," I told him, "but hang onto it and I'll drag you out of here." He didn't want to move. He was in too much pain. "The truck is going to blow. If you don't come with me now, I'll leave you here." He grabbed onto my neck, and I got him up to the highway.

The trucker was crying, and going into shock. He kept wanting to go over to the pickup. I asked the people who pulled up behind me to help him and keep him there. I ran over to help the cop, but there was nothing I could do. The pickup was completely destroyed. There was nothing left of it except for the portion between the headrests and the rear bumper. One of the truck's three occupants was lying on the highway dead. He had flown out the rear window and landed on the road. There was a pool of blood under his head the size of a kitchen table. The cop had his arm inside the wreckage holding a girl's hand. I couldn't believe she was still alive. Just then, the fire rescue truck showed up. I made a quick decision that I didn't want to get caught up in a fatality inquiry. There was nothing more I could do, so I turned around and went back to my car. I got in, did a U-turn, and left.

As I got back to the city, the reality of what had just happened really hit me like a ton of bricks. God had showed me just how quick my life could be taken, but he had given me a second chance! Now it was up to me to show him just what I was going to do with the rest of my life.

I went straight over to my mother's house and told her what had just happened. She was very happy that I wasn't hurt in the accident, but disappointed in me for being weak. "You know you have to leave it in God's hands," she told me. "You have to grow out of this. You are not the only person in this world to have a loved one murdered. The best thing you can do for yourself is read the book of Job. Smarten up!"

Chapter 13

## The Soul's Awakening!

**M**y mother truly is a gift from God. I listened to her advice and read the book of Job. While reading it, I finally saw the big picture and understood what life was really about. This was the definitive focus adjustment I needed. I realized there is a much bigger picture than just what we see in the world. For the first time, my eyes were opened to the spiritual plain, and I clearly saw what was really going on. Thanks, Mom. I love you.

Job was the richest man of his time, and he lived in the land of Uz. He had seven sons and three daughters. His girls were the most beautiful in the land. He owned seven thousand sheep, three thousand camels, one thousand head of cattle, and five hundred donkeys.

One day, there was a meeting in heaven, and the angels appeared before God. God asked Satan, "What have you been doing?"

Satan replied, "I've been roaming around the earth."

God asked Satan about his faithful and trusting servant Job. God said, "No one on earth is as good as him."

"Would Job worship you if you didn't protect him?" Satan replied. "Would he worship you if everything you have given him was taken away?"

"Okay, you can do what you want to him," God said. "But you can't harm Job himself."

Suddenly, the Sabeans attacked one day and stole all Job's oxen and donkeys. Then a lightning storm struck and killed all of his sheep and shepherds. Then bands of Chaldeans attacked and stole all his camels. Finally, all his children were at his oldest son's house when a storm struck and blew the house down, killing them all. In spite of all that, Job did not blame God, but instead praised him. This was Job's first test.

Then there was a second meeting in heaven between God and the angels. God said to Satan, "How is my servant, Job? You've tested him by attacking him for no reason at all, but he is still as faithful as ever."

Satan replied, "Suppose you let me hurt his body. He will curse you forever."

"All right," God said. "You can do anything you want to him, but you can't kill him."

So Satan made Job really sick and put terrible sores all over his body. Before long, Job was living on top of the dung heap garbage pile outside the city walls. Even in all his suffering, Job said nothing against God, and he still worshiped him. But he asked God, "Why are these things happening to me?"

After these two tests, Satan still couldn't break Job's soul. Job held true to God, and the devil lost. Then God blessed Job for standing fast, and he gave him back twice what he had before. In the last part of Job's life, he had fourteen thousand sheep, six thousand camels, two thousand head of cattle, and one thousand donkeys. He was blessed with seven more sons and three more daughters. Job lived for another one hundred and forty years. He lived long enough to see the second set of his great-grandchildren.

After reading the account of Job's life, I was enlightened. I realized what was happening to me. There had been another meeting in heaven at some point, but this time God was talking to the devil about me. Satan claimed that the only reason I didn't kill the men who were responsible for my brother's murder is because God had answered my cry when Lung died of bone cancer. The devil further argued that if I had known exactly who killed my brother, then I would've definitely killed them and become a hypocrite. So, God allowed the devil to test me again. Then Satan let me know exactly who killed my brother and how they murdered him! Like Job, the devil was allowed to do whatever he wanted to me. But he couldn't kill me!

I realized this was why I didn't die in the accident on the highway that day. God didn't let me crash and burn. He was letting the devil put me through the refiner's fire. God rewarded me with his knowledge. If I could have my brother back in exchange for giving up the knowledge the Lord has given me, I wouldn't do it. Why would I want my brother back here in this learning phase when he is with the Lord? I miss him with all my heart, but I can wait to be with him and the Lord. As much as I love my brother, he does not come before the Lord.

Don't get me wrong! I am not trying in any way to compare myself with Job. I am only trying to create a window into the spiritual plain, so that you can see the world as I did. I have been nowhere near as righteous as Job in my life, but we are all tested continually throughout our lives by the devil. Ever since, I've realized that the fight is not carnal. All my life, I was a warrior in my heart, like Peter, the apostle who cut off the slave's ear when they came to arrest Jesus. Jesus healed the slave's ear and told Peter to put his sword away. Well, I am listening to you, my brother, and I am laying down my carnal weapons. I finally understand how you want me to fight this war with Satan. I am putting on the armour of God and will use the most powerful weapon you have given me — your word, the two-edged sword of God, will be my weapon. That is why I am writing this book, my brothers and sisters.

Satan, you lose! I may not be perfect, but I will serve the Lord forever. I love you, God, and thank you for your grace. I thank you for my brother Jesus, and the fruit of the tree of life which he came to share with us. Jesus told the devil when he was being tested in the desert, *"Man does not live on bread alone, but on every word that comes from the mouth of God"* (Matthew 4:4). I understand this now. We need his fruit to live. The word of God truly is the fruit of the tree of life, and the tree of life is the Godhead family. When I was younger, I thought that Christians were wimps for letting themselves be fed to the lions by the Romans. Man, was I ignorant, just like Barabbas, but I didn't understand, because I had the heart of a freedom fighter. Now I understand just how much more courage it takes to walk the walk! Especially unto death, just as Jesus did! These martyrs were quite the act to follow, but we all must endure to the end.

# Chapter 14

## One Final Test

My mother's husband is a retired member of the federal police service. He returned home one day with an illegal unregistered handgun. It was a .32-calibre revolver. He planned to shoot Harley, the lawyer, and he was also going to kill the mole, Sergeant Ratkopitt.

"I'm old and I have nothing to lose," he said. He loved my brother Critter very much and couldn't stand to see them get away with it. I tried to explain to him everything I had learned, but he wouldn't listen. He was raised a Catholic, but he didn't have much faith. He had turned on Jesus. I tried to explain to him that if he denied Christ while he was here, then Jesus would not know him later when he was standing before God. He didn't care and he spoke against the Lord to me.

Jesus said, *"If you tell others that you belong to me, I will then tell my Father in heaven that you are my followers. But if you reject me, I will tell my Father in heaven that you don't belong to me"* (Matthew 10:32–33, CEV). I tried to explain to him that if Critter meant more to him than Jesus did, then the Lord didn't know him. The Lord warned us, *"If you love your father or mother or even your sons and daughters more than me, you are not fit to be my disciples. And unless you are willing to take up your cross and come with me, you are not fit to be my disciples. If you try and save your life, you will lose it. But if you give it up for me, you will surely find it"* (Matthew 10:37–39, CEV). He was too far gone, though. All he wanted was their lives for Critter's. I knew how he felt. I used to be lost and full of hate just like him.

I took it upon myself to disarm him of his weapon. I wasn't sure just what to do with it, because I didn't want to report him to the police. He made threats that he was going to break into my Uncle Rocky's house and steal some guns from him if I didn't give him his gun back. That's when I decided to turn it over to the city police service. I called Detective Given and made arrangements to turn the weapon over to them. Ironically, Detective Style—a schoolmate of my brother Mick—handled it. The police immediately warned these two criminals of his intentions. Over the past year, I never would have believed that I would act in such a way to save their lives. I promptly warned my uncle of his intentions. The police charged him, but the prosecutor's office later dropped all the charges. The police told me, "The prosecutor's office dropped all the charges because of his age, his health, his service, and the circumstances." I don't think they did him any favours. I believe they did it in order to avoid any public embarrassment to the criminal justice system. I never spoke with him again after that. My mother promptly separated from him, and then he died in a quad accident. I don't know if he ever made his peace with God.

# Part Three

# Light for the Wheat

## Chapter 15

## The Lampstand

Light is the knowledge given to men by God if they are so fortunate in this life. Many prophets, from the time of Adam to when Jesus came, wanted to hear the words of God. When Eve convinced Adam to eat the fruit of the tree of knowledge of good and evil, mankind was cut off from the fruit of the tree of life. The fruit of the tree of knowledge of good and evil is the secular, godless knowledge of this world, and it comes straight from the devil. Very few prophets, from the time of Adam until Jesus came, received the word of God. Many longed for it, though. When Jesus shared the light in the parables with us, he was giving us access to the fruit of the tree of life again.

If you are wise, then listen, my brothers and sisters. If you can see, then use your eyes to study the parables, for they are the word of God. The Catholic hierarchy would not publish the word of God for centuries. During that time, the common man could not read it for himself. Also, they only spoke God's word in Latin, and the common man could not understand it. This was done intentionally as a means of exercising control over the people. The Protestants knew this and broke away from the Catholics. They started to print the Bible, so that all men could read it for themselves. In this day and age, we have no excuse not to read the Bible, so study the parables. The application of their truth is timeless. The parables were the truth when Jesus first spoke them, just as they are today, and they will be forever. Wake up and save your soul! Spread the good news to all the corners of the earth, like our brother Jesus has commanded us.

If you are given light from the Lord, then this is your lamp. There is a parable about the lamp. The Lord told us, *"No one lights a lamp and puts it under a bowl or under a bed. A lamp is always put on a lampstand, so that people who come into a house will see the light"* (Luke 8:16, CEV).

I know now that I have been commissioned by my brother Jesus to do this! Jesus said, *"Pay attention to how you listen! Everyone who has something will be given more, but people who have nothing will lose what little they think they have"* (Luke 8:18, CEV).

He also said, *"Whatever I say to you in the dark, you must tell in the light. And you must announce from the housetops whatever I have whispered to you"* (Matthew 10:27, CEV). I understand, my brother! You have instructed me to take up my cross and follow you. Jesus said, *"Unless you are willing to take up your cross and come with me, you are not fit to be my disciples. If you try to save your life, you will lose it. But if you give it up for me, you will surely find it"* (Mathew 10: 38-39, CEV). I know that you do not want me to bury the gold you have given me. I will follow your direction and give it to the poor. Thank you for entrusting me with your gold, my brother (see Luke 19:11-27).

All the things which I have been through, because of my brother's murder, are my cross. Each of us in this world has our own cross to bear. I hope that by sharing mine I can help other victims. I want to help other people struggling with vengeance to make the right choices. The violence of this world must stop. It's up to each of us to stop it. We can't control what others do, not even our own children, but we can be an example for others. Just stop the violence by controlling yourself!

The most important thing I want to do before I die is please my Maker. I fear that he will be ashamed that he has created me. I want him to be pleased with the way in which I have chosen to live. Even with all the mistakes I have made throughout my life, I know he forgives me and that he loves me. All I have to do is learn from my mistakes and do what he wants me to do. God's eternal gift to men is his grace. I want him to be glad that he has made me.

I pray, "Father, please forgive those men who murdered my brother Critter. For they are blind and ignorant, and they do not know what they have done. They have choked out some of your wheat. I pray they will wake up before they die and turn to you for forgiveness. I hope they will truly repent and follow your ways, for their own good. I leave them in your trust, my Father. Amen."

It has been many years now since my soul's awakening, but I still remember that first moment. It was as though Atlas had the globe removed from his back! When you follow Jesus, his yoke truly is light. Jesus said, *"If you are tired from carrying heavy burdens, come to me and I will give you rest. Take the yoke I give you.*

*Put it on your shoulders and learn from me, I am gentle and humble, and you will find rest. This yoke is easy to bear, and this burden light"* (Matthew 11:28-30, CEV). Jesus stands knocking at the door to your heart, mind, and soul. If you hear him knocking, open the door and let him in. He will never leave you! Amen. I know this truth! He was there for me in the darkest hour of my life! I am my brother's living witness.

For over twelve years, I have used the analogy of a police dog. If a dog does not listen to its handler, what good is it? If a dog's master gives it a command, it must obey the command to be useful. I am the dog, and God is my master. God has commanded me to stay and to stand fast. For years now, I have stood fast, but I still growl intensely at these murderers! I've said many times over the years that if God finally gave me permission to weed his field, I would really enjoy hunting them down and taking them out. All he needed to say was, "Sick 'em, Dano," and thy will be done—immediately!

Even with all the knowledge the Lord has given me, I still didn't understand completely. Sure, I was standing fast, and I wouldn't think of physically going after them unless God ordered me to… but what a hypocrite I still was, and I didn't even know it. In my heart and mind, I still desired my pound of flesh. I finally realized while writing this paragraph that I was a mental hypocrite. I was no better than the chief priests of the temple Jesus had warned us about. Jesus taught us that if you are married and you remain physically faithful to your wife, but you still look at another woman and want her in your mind, then you are just as guilty as if you committed the physical act (see Matthew 5:28). In other words, according to this school of thought, I was just as guilty in front of the Lord as if I had taken them out, and I didn't even know it! I had absolutely no idea how dead I was for all these years, because I still wanted to take out these scumbags in my heart and mind. In criminal law, guilt is proven two ways — by *actus reus* and *mens rea*. In other words, you are guilty by the act of committing a crime or you are guilty by the criminal intent to commit the crime. I didn't have the intent, but I sure was obsessed with the desire for his permission to execute the act!

As I was writing these last few paragraphs, God spoke to me and woke me up. I was blind and I couldn't see this for years! The light finally came on in my mind, and now I can see clearly. This is how the Lord speaks to me. I'm not some kind of religious nut! I can't stand manmade religions. That's not what it's all about! We definitely don't learn everything in one day. I can finally see that the Peter part of my natural born character was still pulling me down. Satan still had a part of my soul, and I didn't even know it. Thank you for letting me realize this, Lord. I truly have forgiven them now. It has been a long hard road to this point! I no longer have any desire to hunt them down and take them out. I want nothing more than to steal their souls back from the devil. This is the real war! The Lord has sent us out as sheep amongst the wolves. We all must be on our toes, one hundred percent of the time, because we are doing battle with the craftiest of evil. Beware of the dark light of this world, for it's one of the most powerful weapons of Satan.

# Chapter 16

# The Cookie Jar

In this life, we are born naturally into sin. This is a fact because of what Adam and Eve did when they chose not to listen to God. They chose to listen to that snake and go their own way. The rest of the human race has paid the price for their decision ever since. When we are born, we live by our natural instincts. We all want to survive. We will fight for that right to survive. Self-preservation is an innate, natural-born instinct of every species on the planet, but vengeance is not. Take a tiger in the wild, for instance. A mother tiger is off hunting to feed her cubs. When she returns, she finds that one of her cubs has been killed. The mother tiger will not innately go after whatever has killed her cub. Now, if she is present when something threatens her cubs, that's a different story. She will fight that threat to the death.

Life is funny. It is full of all kinds of learning experiences and tests, right from the cookie jar to who we really are... inside.

For instance, you're a three-year-old child watching your mother bake cookies. When she's done, you naturally want some, but she won't let you have any. She puts them away in the cookie jar. She has her reasons for not letting you have any. It will spoil your appetite for supper, but you are not conscious of this. All you want is some cookies. Off she goes to do some laundry, and while she's gone, you get a chair. You slide the chair over to the counter and climb up. You open the jar and take some of the cookies out. This was your first test by the devil, and you failed. You don't even know that Satan has tested you and won. Just like Adam and Eve, you did what you wanted. This is the devil's way, and this is what Satan wants you to do. This is when he likes to attack us, when we are not conscious of it. If you are lucky, you will get caught by your mother, and she will give you some form of negative reinforcement so that you will learn.

I remember my first test experience. It wasn't with cookies, nor was it with my mother. It was with chocolate ex-lax. I was staying at the lake one summer with my grandmother. I was about four years old. One morning, I saw her eating what looked like some chocolate. I asked her, "Can I have some?"

"It's not chocolate," she told me. "It's medicine. I can't give you any because it will make you sick." She put it way up high on the top of her bedroom clothes closet. While she was outside working in her garden, I got a chair. I climbed up and took the box down. I ate just about the whole thing. I thought I was pretty smart. I left a little bit to make it look like I hadn't touched it. I put the rest back exactly where it was, and then I put the chair back.

Within an hour, I was running back and forth to the outhouse for the rest of the day. I remember my grandmother watching me going back and forth all day. She never said a word to me, but she had this little smile on her face that I remember to this day. She knew exactly what I had done. I should have listened to her, but my desire for the chocolate was too great. She had never lied to me, and I knew she loved me very much. She just let nature take its course, and believe me, I learned quickly never to doubt her again. I now know why I didn't listen to her. It's because I was being tested by Satan, for the first time. Man, did I fail! Believe me, it was a real crappy experience!

Over the next couple of years, I learned what laxatives were and what they are used for. One day at school, I had my first taste of revenge. It was around Halloween, and I remember eating some Chiclets gum. This older bully-type kid came along and wanted some. I refused to give him any because I didn't know him from Adam. Then he grabbed my pack of gum and took some anyway. Well, that night I came up with an idea! I took a full box of ex-lax gum and put it into a Chiclets gum box. I filled the whole box with laxatives except for the first row. I went to school the next day and purposely baited this kid. My buddy and I went right up beside this bully and I pulled out my gum. I gave my friend some real gum, and I ate some, too. Then this bully came up to us, and he wanted some. This time I didn't hesitate and gave him the whole box. He grabbed a big handful and threw them into his mouth. He thought he was pretty smart. He figured he had intimidated me. He gave me the box back with only one or two pieces left in it.

I remember thinking how sweet it was getting my revenge. I didn't get to watch him running to the toilet all day because I was in class, but I remember laughing with my buddy about what I had done. This bully never said anything to me about it. I don't think he was smart enough to figure out what I had done to him. Oh well, I got the last laugh. Or did I? No, I didn't, because Satan actually did. I wanted my revenge, and I got it. Satan won that day. He got the real last laugh on me, and I didn't even know it.

Hopefully we learn from life's lessons before it's too late. Life unravels like the string theory the Lord has given me. When we are born, our timeline starts and there is a peg used to mark our birthdate. Only God knows how long our life will be. God attaches a string to this peg, and the length of this string is the length of our lives. In the beginning, the string is crisscrossing, and it goes all over the place. The string's path is like this because God pulls it tight before we are born, and then releases it when we enter this world. Then the string has no certain direction, and it goes everywhere erratically. Thus, we are naturally born into sin. This simulates the event of when Adam and Eve disobeyed God, and they broke their strings with him. Then they were kicked out of the garden of Eden. As we live our lives, God starts to tug on our string again. These tugs represent the times when he is calling us, when we are being tested in life. Each time God tugs on our string, he pulls us closer to him. Eventually our paths become straighter.

You have probably heard the saying that the road to hell is paved with good intentions. Well, it's true. Jesus told us, *"Go in through the narrow gate. The gate to destruction is wide, and the road that leads there is easy to follow. A lot of people go through that gate. But the gate to life is very narrow. The road that leads there is so hard to follow that only a few people find it"* (Matthew 7:13–14, CEV). The path of the road and the path of your string are the same thing. If you resist God each time he tugs on your string, eventually there will be so much tension that your string will break.

That's what the devil wants. Satan wants you to resist God, and he wants you to break your string. Then he has won. So if you are wise, pay attention when God is tugging on your string, and walk the narrow path in life! Believe me, if you listen, the path does get straighter and straighter as you get older. Which path in life is easier to follow? A straight line, or one that goes all over the place chaotically? The Lord is a fisher of men, so if you feel him tugging on your string, let him reel you in. This is what it's all about—letting the Lord catch you and not letting the devil break your string.

# Chapter 17

# The Double Cross

In Jesus' day, the holy men of the temple believed that cleanliness was next to Godliness. So they would take two baths a day and change their clothes several times as well. They would not think of eating any unclean food. Jesus said, *"What goes into a man's mouth does not make him 'unclean,' but what comes out of his mouth, that is what makes him 'unclean'"* (Matthew 15:10–11). *"I promise you that on the day of judgment, everyone will have to account for every careless word they have spoken"* (Matthew 12:36). God knows what is truly in the hearts and minds of men. You will be judged by every word you say in this life. These self-righteous men would never commit adultery once they were married. At the same time, when they would see a beautiful young woman, they would fantasize about what they would do with her. As far as Jesus was concerned they had already committed adultery in their minds (see Matthew 5:27–28). We must apply these fundamental principles of truth in every area of our lives, so that we do not become like these men. They were blind, mental hypocrites. If you live your life by these teachings, you will earn the respect of your fellow man and the confidence of the Lord! But if you do not, then you are already dead.

Over the centuries the devil has been working really hard to disprove creation, discredit Christianity, and attack the books of the Bible. His attempts have incorporated many forms, right from the so-called science of evolution to modern-day organizations like the Zeitgeist movement. Satan is very cunning and resourceful in his evil! His greatest achievement has been convincing people that he isn't real and that he doesn't even exist. Don't be fooled by this! He is definitely real, and he is actively trying to destroy mankind! This is what he's all about! Some of the greatest damage he has been able to inflict on mankind comes from within Christendom's manmade churches. The continued blatant hypocrisy of these so-called Christian churches has been one of Satan's most effective tools over the centuries!

Many different mediums, such as books, films, and television shows have been created in order to try to discredit the Bible. For example, *The Da Vinci Code*, a work of fiction. This story tries to rewrite the life of Jesus, claiming that he had a child with Mary Magdalene. I'm sure that one of the authors of the four gospels would have recorded this fact if it were true, don't you think? Anyway, what's more important? Whether Jesus had a child, or the words of truth he gave us? Think about it! He came to teach us and adjust our focus, not leave us his heir. They use this malarkey in an attempt to divert our attention from the Lord's word!

It really troubles me to see the books of the Bible being attacked on television. I've seen a lot of science documentaries that try to disprove creation and promote evolution. A basic understanding of genetics proves that there is evolution within a species itself. If a species does not adapt to its environment over time, it will die out. However, there is no definitive proof that a species evolves from one into another, even though this is totally accepted as fact in the scientific community today. Actually, it's quite the contrary. There are nothing but missing links — not just the one between man and apes. You don't have to look any further than mules. Sure, you can breed two different types of species like donkeys and horses... but their offspring are sterile! This simple fact of genetics proves that evolution only takes place within a species itself. I can't believe that some of these so-called scientists are still trying to convince us that we have come from apes and monkeys. Sure, we share the same DNA building blocks, but we were never the same! This is what I call the science of *evilution*! Do not be misled by this malarkey even though they allow it to be taught in our secular schools along with creation.

We have always been individually created, just as we individually die out and become extinct. For example, man invented ships that cross the oceans and planes that cross the skies. They share the same basic construction of metal frames and skins. They are both held together by nuts and bolts, and each is powered by an engine. Similarly, they can both be automatically piloted by computers, but one did not evolve out of the other. These are totally separate inventions with their own unique designs, even though they share the same building blocks. Sure, you can try to group them together and call them both ships.

The latest and greatest of these ships are spaceships, like the space shuttle. This is also a totally separate invention. This is why there are patents which are protected by the law. The law states that they each share similar technologies, but are separate inventions. Are the lawyers smarter and more evolved than the scientists? I know… the one grew out of the other.

The Zeitgeist movement makes a lot of unsubstantiated claims about Christianity and Jesus. It's easy to say that Jesus didn't really exist, and that the facts of his life are just a bunch of myths taken from other civilizations' religions. But they have made these claims without providing any specific reference material relating to proven historical facts. Clearly all they have done is make unfounded associations. None of their statements can be quickly validated through researching their references because they don't have any! Every quality paper ever published contains these. A curious fact is that I've never seen any of these organizations, their books, films or television programs try to challenge the word of God. I am referring specifically to the parables which Jesus taught us while he was here. Satan is really trying hard to use all these different mediums to attack God and Christianity, but none of them have tried to attack the word of God! How can you attack the truth? The truth is timeless, and it will never change! It is the two-edged sword of God that will cut through their lies, and they know it. You can't argue with the truth! This is why you never see a program that tries to attack the word of God!

The Lord hates hypocrisy more than anything! The seditious hypocrisy of the Catholic Church's incorporation of secular reasoning has corrupted the commandments of God, and the true principles of Christianity for over eighteen centuries. Their institutional practice of this evil, and the subliminal influence it's had over the world for centuries is the great double cross of Christianity. It must stop! Jesus came here in the flesh to adjust the focus of men, because we just weren't getting it. We didn't get it then, over two thousand years ago when he first tried to teach us, and we still don't today. The Catholic Church claims to be the only true Christian church of God. Well, I don't know where the current pope gets this malarkey from, because he's dead wrong. Jesus told us, *"Whenever two or three of you come together in my name, I am there with you"* (Matthew 18:20, CEV). Make no mistake, this is the true church of our Lord! Real church is anywhere two or more people gather in his name to share the truth he has given us! It's definitely not a building, or an individual, self-righteous, manmade religion!

The Catholic Church is guilty of not practicing true Christianity for over eighteen centuries, and that is why the Protestant movement started. This church has been engendering Christian hypocrisy from its beginning. Since the time of Constantine they have been backing wars in the name of Christendom. They had monks who were warrior knights who fought in all the crusades in the name of God. God didn't instruct them to do that, and he surely didn't want them to do that. They have been promoting war from their inception. When God wants us to fight a war in his name, he will tell us! God didn't have Moses rise up in war and fight the Egyptians, but he definitely instructed Joshua to go to war. The Catholic Church murdered and tortured all kinds of people throughout the inquisition, and used the confessional for blackmail. Mussolini, the Italian fascist dictator of the Second World War, was baptized as a Catholic in 1927. Most mafioso are devoted Catholics who commit murder or contract killings, and they are accepted as Catholic Church members. I guess they're forgiven every Friday for who they've killed during the week, assuming their tithes are great enough.

The Swiss banking corporations have succumbed to the pressure applied by many world organizations to return the gold and money deposited by the Jewish holocaust victims. The same thing should be done to the Vatican's corporations! I challenge the world's justice institutions to make the Catholic Church give back all the gold and money they've taken from the indigenous people of the Americas during the last five centuries! Do you have any idea how much gold was taken by force from the natives of Mexico, and the nations of Central and South America? This so-called church should be ashamed of itself for raping these nations of their gold and money in the name of Christianity!

Constantine, the head of the Roman Empire, saw a cross in the sky. He believed this was a sign from Christ. Constantine believed that Christ wanted him to fight all of his battles in his name. He obviously knew nothing about Jesus. Constantine was just another ignorant, secular warrior. He has gone down in history as the original Catholic hypocrite. Around the year 313 A.D., Constantine adopted Christianity as the new state religion of the Roman Empire. This religion was manmade and is now known as Catholicism; it is an adulterated form of true Christianity. Constantine's religion was based on Christianity, but this Romanism has gone its own way throughout history. They just traded in the ranks of the Roman Legions for the Catholic hierarchy. Christianity should be a way of life in the service of people, period! Jesus doesn't want anyone to fight wars in his name! He didn't then, and he doesn't now! Jesus instructed us to love our enemies and to turn the other cheek. He said, *"When someone slaps your right cheek, turn and let that person slap your other cheek. If someone sues you for your shirt, give up your coat as well. If a soldier forces you to carry his pack one mile, carry it two miles... You have heard people say, 'Love your neighbors and hate your enemies.' But I tell you to love your enemies and pray for anyone who mistreats you. Then you will be acting like your Father in heaven"* (Matthew 5:39–41, 43–45, CEV). He did not leave the door open to any exceptions, period! There are no ifs, ands or buts. Jesus did not support Barabbas in his fight against the Romans!

Does this sound like a man who wants you to fight wars in his name? Definitely not! This is why I don't understand why contemporary pastors like Billy Graham have supported the military forces since World War II... don't they get it? Once you truly understand Jesus, how can you support secular wars or violence for any reason without being a hypocrite? Unless these pastors' intentions were to work with the sick, as Jesus did. When Jesus overheard the Pharisees accuse him of associating with sinners and the tax collectors, he answered them, *"Healthy people don't need a doctor, but sick people do. Go and learn what the scriptures mean when they say, 'Instead of offering sacrifices to me, I want you to be merciful to others.' I didn't come to invite good people to be my followers. I came to invite sinners,"* (Matthew 9:11-13, CEV).

Billy Graham is considered to be a modern-day prophet. He has brought millions of people to the Lord by teaching them about John 3:16. Billy mentors them on how to be born again. Near the end of the Second World War he joined the American military after completing his pastoral training. How can you be a real Christian and serve in the military? You can't! It's impossible to serve God and the military. It's an oxymoron! Like, living death! It just doesn't make any sense! The two are oil and water and they can never mix! Think about it!

If you're a pastor and a soldier you could easily encounter an active combat situation where, under orders, you would have to fight and kill the enemy. If you chose not to follow orders, but instead held true to your Christian principles you would face a court-martial and the firing squad. Nice! Die fighting for them, or be executed for refusing to kill for them! This is why we must be conscientious objectors. Let the dead police the dead with their own hypocrisy. Let them use the godless Rambos of this world to do their killing for them. We have a far more important battle to worry about!

Billy went to the front lines in Korea to support the American troops. Why has no one challenged this way of thinking? Am I the only one who can see something wrong with this school of thought? It seems apparent to me that this form of Christian hypocrisy has been carried over from Catholicism to the protestant movement. Jesus made it very clear! We are not to fight in wars for any reason! There are no exceptions! This evil darkness has been thriving for over eighteen centuries. There is no sitting on the fence! We must be conscientious objectors and set the example. We have to stop encouraging the lost who are fighting in these wars, otherwise we are hypocrites! We cannot condone the violence of this world or fighting for any reason. It must stop! You cannot meet violence with violence, it only creates more violence! Sure, the evil men of this world can knock you around. They can even kick you while you're down, but do not return their violence with violence! As long as you know they can only harm your body, and they can never touch your soul, then they can only beat you, but they can never defeat you! When you remain humble, and do not meet their aggression with force, then it triggers something deep with in the human spirit. Once they experience this self-humiliation they immediately know that what they are doing is dead wrong, and they will stop! Gandhi knew this and he had it right when he instructed his people to do nothing when they were attacked with violence. He said, "Just sit it out, and they'll go away!" Guess what? They did!

The first Irish Catholic President of the United States was a true Christian hypocrite. It's common knowledge that he committed adultery numerous times. Another accepted fact is that he sanctioned the CIA to assassinate Fidel Castro at least three times. The dictionary's definition of assassination is to murder in a sudden, secret attack. Castro never did anything to Kennedy! He never attacked the United States, and he never planned to! In 1962, President Kennedy and his Joint Chiefs of Staff planned an act of homeland terrorism against the United States! This is known as a false flag operation. It was planned that this attack would be blamed on Cuba and Fidel Castro. President Kennedy claimed to have been a Christian. I ask you, how could he order the murder of another country's leader and be a real Christian? His own actions have just proven him to be another hypocrite of history. The Bible says that if you live by the sword, you will die by the sword. Ironically, he was assassinated. Was this scripture being proven to man again? I definitely do not support any form of communism or hypocrisy!

War is a product of the secular world, and it usually involves greed and power. Believe me, wars are fought in the name of all kinds of things, but the real reasons are always the same. Jesus instructed us to love our enemies. He did not want us to fight with them and kill them. He said, *"If you only love those around you, what reward will you get? Are not even the tax collectors doing that? And if you greet only your brothers, what are you doing more than others? Do not even pagans do that? Be perfect, therefore, as your heavenly Father is perfect"* (Matthew 5:46–48). The Christians who were fed to the lions by the Romans knew this, and that is why they let themselves be murdered. They walked the walk, just as Jesus did! They weren't all mouth, and just a bunch of phony hypocrites. These men and women were true martyrs of Christianity. I'm curious to know, when all is said and done, just how many of these so-called Catholic Christians actually walked this walk in life? Peter couldn't even do this and he's supposed to be their first pope. If the pope is supposed to be on the same level as Jesus, then why does he need a bullet-proof vehicle and Swiss guards? Where is his faith?

Jesus doesn't want any of us fighting each other, especially for the reasons of men. We are not to be like Barabbas, or Osama Bin Laden! We are not to be freedom fighters or peacekeepers! God blesses the peacemakers, not men of violence! None of these men's reasons are justified in the eyes of the Lord! The only thing we are to fight for while here on earth is God's way, and our weapons are not of this world. We are instructed to use the word of God.

Many people believe that Jesus came to bring peace to the world, but he did not! He came to wake us up and adjust the focus of man in the world. He wants to save us from ourselves, because we are just blind, ignorant, hypocrites! He came to turn brother against brother, and mother against daughter. This is what happens when one of them believes what he says and the other does not accept it (see Matthew 10:34-37). I am perfectly aware that some of you will not accept what I am telling you, but that's okay because your cups are full, and you are not meant to. You are full of preconceived convictions. I used to think just like you, before God enlightened me! To accept the word of God, you must become like a young child. A child's cup is not full of learned convictions yet! It is empty. Their ears are open and they hear the message clearly. Out of the mouth of babes comes the truth, so listen to them.

## Chapter 18

## The Black Light

I warn you! You must be on guard against the black light of this world. It is a wolf in sheep's clothing. If you choose to accept these secular lies as truth, you will surely die. I know from personal experience, because I was dead. You must challenge the false doctrine of the secular leaders of this evil world! If you choose to live on their misguided knowledge alone, it will be like putting the head of an infant in the mouth of a wild lion.

When 9/11 happened, President Bush went in front of the news cameras and said, "We are at war with terrorists. Either you are with us or you are with the terrorists." I have never heard anything so ludicrous! I guess his vocabulary is very limited. It obviously doesn't include the words "neutral" or "separate." I personally don't want anything to do with the terrorists, or President Bush! I am definitely not sitting on the fence, and this is not a black and white issue. Who is Bush to force this ultimatum on me, or anyone else in this world? His words are pure evil and he sounds clearly like a dictator to me. This is an example of the black light which I am warning you about!

Jesus answered this malarkey in his day by saying, *"Anyone who isn't against us is for us"* (Mark 9:40, CEV). He also said, *"If you are not on my side, you are against me. If you don't gather in the harvest with me, you scatter it"* (Matthew 12:30, CEV). Can you see the difference? Bush's words are far more than a matter of poor speech or semantics. Jesus said, *"I know everything you have done, and you are not cold or hot. I wish you were either one or the other. But since you are lukewarm and neither cold nor hot, I will spit you out of my mouth"* (Revelation 3:15–16, CEV). There is no sitting on the fence. I have always been an all-or-nothing type of person. That's why I want nothing to do with either side. Two wrongs do not make a right! That's why I must choose to be a conscientious objector.

Bush ordered his forces to attack two countries that did not attack the United States. He said, "Whether we bring our enemies to justice or justice to our enemies, justice will be done!" These acts of war are unfounded. They are clearly not acts of justice, but outright vengeance disguising their real ulterior motives! He started these so-called wars in Afghanistan and Iraq illegally. What he has done is dead wrong! He attacked and invaded them. Where does he think he gets the right to do this? It sure isn't from the Lord's word, as he implies, or by any existing authority under international law. God did not appoint him to police the world, and neither did the rest of the world's leaders! This evil doctrine comes straight from the fruit of the tree of the knowledge of good and evil! This is a pure example of the secular evil of this world which I am warning you about!

President Bush claims to be a Christian, but he obviously doesn't know the first thing about being a real Christian. Nothing's changed in the presidency in over fifty years. He's just another hypocrite president with ulterior motives. He put a twenty-five million dollar death bounty on Osama Bin Laden. When Bush received a report that his forces had killed Bin Laden, he immediately ordered his men to bring him the head of Osama. It turned out not to be the head of Osama Bin Laden. Who does president think he is... a modern-day King Herod? This is definitely not the way to get ahead in life! No pun intended. Bush said, "We will rid the world of evildoers!" He thinks he's a harvest worker, and that he has the right to weed God's field. You're definitely no angel, George! Jesus does not want us to eradicate our enemies! He made it very clear that we are not to do this! These statements are clearly the evil semantics of an Antichrist. The Lord said, *"Not everyone who calls me their Lord will get into the kingdom of heaven. Only the ones who obey my Father in heaven will get in… But I will tell them, 'I will have nothing to do with you! Get out of my sight, you evil people!'"* (Matthew 7:21, 23, CEV).

Bush claims to be a good friend of Billy Graham. If this is true, then I'd say it's high time to wake him up, Billy. I don't believe he has completely read the Bible once. If he had, how could he be so ignorant and act so evil? God didn't tell President Bush to go to war. Bush and his gang had their own reasons to create these wars. His new world order crusade—excuse me, I mean his so-called "War on Terrorism." The 9/11 attacks had absolutely nothing to do with Iraq or Saddam Hussein. Bush and his cohorts had their own ulterior motives—like oil, greed, and revenge. There were no weapons of mass destruction in

Iraq as he claimed, and none were ever found. So why did Bush really attack them? Think about it. History has proven him and his gang to be liars. The leaders of Britain, Canada, and the rest of the coalition just followed him like little sheep. Don't these leaders have any critical thinking skills of their own? At least Canada didn't follow them into Iraq. Many other nations were asked to join his coalition and conscientiously declined! The co-alition is just a gang of nations doing what they want. It's a good thing China and a few other nations decided not to stop the coalition forces! Do you have any idea how many Muslims live in China? Most Muslims are from the Far East; only about ten percent of them are Arabs.

There are four types of men in this world—not just good men and bad men. First, there are the good-good guys, like Jesus and the prophets. Also, some common men throughout history like Noah, Lot, and Job fall into this category. Not many of us can live up to this high standard of men. Maybe Gandhi or a few other men of peace can. Second, there are the bad-bad guys who are pure evil, like psychopaths. There has been no lack of these evil weeds, such as Hitler and Osama Bin Laden, since the beginning of mankind. Third, there are the bad-good guys, who are the hypocrites—like dirty cops and vigilante murdering leaders. They present themselves to be one thing, but they are really something else. Finally, there are the good-bad guys, like Robin Hood and Jesse James. I don't know about you, but I'd rather be a good-bad guy than a bad-good guy any day of the week! At least you're not a hypocrite and the world will know you're a straight shooter. There's a rhyme that says, "I'm the king of the castle, and you're the dirty rascal." It all depends on who's in power. Was Robin Hood the dirty rascal or Prince

John? Propaganda plays a big role in this world, but God knows the truth. Who was evil? Jesse James or the Pinkerton enforcers who worked for the railroad as hired guns? Think about it! Was it the mercenaries of the old west or both? Definitely both!

The ones paying the price for this malarkey are the young brainwashed men and women serving in the forces. They think they are peacekeepers, and they believe that they are serving their country. These are some of the people I am trying to convey this message to for my brother. So please, wake up! The last thing I want to do is to offend any of you veterans, but you must challenge this evil mentality. These young men and women are prepared to make the ultimate sacrifice and lay down their lives for their country. Is this really the ultimate act of bravery? Is this really what they are doing? I don't think so! I know it isn't! But it sure is what the ruling establishment wants to mislead their peacekeepers into believing. Walk away! Let them use the Godless Rambos of their secular world to do it for them. Let the dead police the dead! Don't let them use you for their ulterior motives.

The real people who control the nations of the world are not the puppet leaders who are put into power. No, it's really the richest and most powerful men behind the scenes, like the members of the American Enterprises Institute and the Bilderberg Group. Who's really calling the shots? The little protestant crusader, or the big Dick behind Halliburton! Wake up! It's always been this way. You will never see any of these evil men personally fight in the wars which they create. No, they are far too smart for that; they'll just use you to do it for them. So, wake up! Listen to the Lord, and have nothing to do with their evil!

Listen up and pay attention, you young peacekeepers, who believe that there is no greater thing than to lay down your life for your brother. Jesus is the one who said this, but the concept of modern-day warfare and enforcement is definitely not what he meant by it. My Uncle Rocky believed this malarkey. He was conditioned to this way of thinking while serving in the Navy during the Second World War. Police officers are also misled into believing that this saying glorifies dying in the line of duty. The secular world has perverted this saying! They have become experts at twisting its true meaning. This is what Jesus truly meant when he said this! You must give up your own way of life and your own way of thinking. You must follow him in his ways and then you will truly become born again. You must embrace a life in the service of others.

After the war, my Uncle Rocky joined the fire department. When firefighters lay down their lives in the line of duty, as so many did on 9/11, then indeed this saying applies. There is no enforcement involved while saving lives and property! They gave up their lives while helping their fellow man, not while killing them for the current establishment. Have you ever heard of the richest and most powerful men fighting a war for their country? Definitely not! That's why Bush tactfully avoided going to Vietnam during his military service! He just stayed home, all nice and safe, and only played at being an Air Force pilot in his own backyard. This is how he really obtained his veteran status. He sure wallowed in his glory when he showed up on the carrier in the Gulf. He was just playing the role of Texas Ranger of the world. God did not appoint him top cop of the world!

There are so many cases of friendly fire incidents during war. Friendly fire is when a soldier kills another soldier who is on the same side as himself. Two American fighter pilots dropped a 500-pound bomb on Canadian soldiers in this so-called war on terrorism! Four of these soldiers were killed and eight more were seriously wounded! It is believed that these pilots were using clinical speed when they targeted these Canadian soldiers! A drug called dexamphetamine which is prescribed to them by their military's doctors! The American Air Force issues these drugs to their pilots so they can stay alert while on long missions. How can they justify doing this? Meanwhile, back at home, the American government is fighting a war on drugs, like speed! These~drugs like rock cocaine, crack and methamphetamine~are all known as speeders. Talk about pure hypocrisy committed by the American government!

Oh, I understand! They pretend to follow the rules in their own backyard. But in reality, they do whatever they want everywhere including their own backyard! They send their country's young men off to war stoned on drugs so they can kill the enemy faster and more efficiently for longer periods of time, and then they call them heroes. Meanwhile, back at home, if some poor drug addict gets caught with speed or kills someone accidentally while stoned on it, they go to the penitentiary. Am I the only one who can see something wrong with this picture? Is everyone blind? Do you have any idea the amount of drugs the American Armed Forces used in Vietnam? It's a sad, sad thing!

The people of Iraq and Afghanistan didn't ask for the coalition's help. These countries did not attack the United States or declare war against them. A fanatical cell of Muslim extremists with perverted religious values did! Wars are fought between nations, and not between a group of nations and a small band of evil terrorists, who all died in the 9/11 attacks! Bush described the actions of the coalition as a "War on Terrorism." This was a very effective use of semantics to disguise their real ulterior motives. Call it want you want, but it's still dead wrong on both sides!

We still don't get it! Nothing's changed in over two thousand years. Osama Bin Laden thought he was some kind of modern-day Barabbas fighting for the Muslim world, against the modern-day Romans. What he calls, "The evil United States of America." The coalition forces invaded these countries with no international legal authority and deposed their governments. Who appointed them to do that? It sure wasn't God, Jesus or the rest of the world! Yes. Osama Bin Laden did publicly take credit for the attacks of 9/11, but how does that justify these two wars Bush started; and what does 9/11 have to do with the invasion of these two sovereign nations? Absolutely nothing! No, they had their ulterior motives and exercised them.

President Bush and his cohorts did exactly what they wanted to do, despite what the rest of the world had to say. The United Nations did not agree with the coalition's actions or support them. President Bush has acted like the bully of the world, and by his own actions he has shown his true colors. History has definitely taught us that the weak will gang up and take down the strong. President Bush is not practicing Christianity as a way of life, or as the leader of a so-called Christian nation. Whether his actions are premeditated or pure ignorance, it doesn't matter. Hypocrisy is hypocrisy! It's easy to claim to be a Christian leader, but it's another thing to make righteous decisions as one. We will all be judged by what we have done in this life, and also by the shallow misleading words that come out of our mouths! President Bush is going down in history as the first crusading protestant leader. This little president sure has a lot to be proud of! He has put America in huge debt. The States' war debt, incurred by his decisions, has greatly contributed to the world's latest financial crisis. You can't keep spending trillions of dollars on war, for almost a decade, and not burst the bubble.

Chapter 19

# The Lord's Mirror

Mr. President, Jesus instructed me to share his fruit with you, so that your eyes may be opened too! When you are walking in the darkness of this world, how can you see the evil you have done? How can you lead your nation through the darkness when you yourself are blind? The blind cannot lead the blind! This message is the light which I have received from the Lord. I am putting it on the lampstand, so that you and others may find your way through the darkness of this evil world (see Matthew 5:13-16). All that is hidden will be known, so if you have any wisdom wake up and pay attention! Listen carefully to what the Lord wants me to tell you... because the sky will fall one day!

King David saw a very beautiful woman one day from his palace roof while she was taking a bath. David had to know who she was, because he wanted her. Her name was Bathsheba, the wife of Uriah. David sent for her, and then made love to her. Bathsheba became pregnant by David. David sent her husband Uriah to the front lines of the war they were fighting, so that he would be killed. Uriah was intentionally put in harm's way by David so that he could have his wife.

God then sent Nathan the prophet to give David a message. Nathan told David about two men who lived in the same town. One man was very rich, with lots of cattle and sheep. The other man was very poor, and he only had one little lamb. He loved his lamb very much, like it was his own child. He even fed his little lamb exactly what he ate. The rich man had a visitor one day, and he didn't want to use one of his own animals for the meal. Instead, he took the poor man's only lamb and prepared it. David became very mad at the rich man after hearing what he had done! He said, "I swear by the living God that this man should die for what he has done! He must pay back four times for doing such a cruel thing!" Then Nathan told David, "You are that man! You had Uriah killed in battle, and you took his wife. You have sinned greatly against the Lord."

The police chief of the city of San Diego had his family murdered one day. His family were the victims of a home invasion, and they were blown up! These criminals were attempting to set a bomb, so that it would go off at a later time when the chief was at home. They accidentally triggered the bomb while trying to set it. They killed themselves along with the chief's family. The chief knew exactly who had killed his family and why. It was a Mexican drug lord who sent his men to blow up the chief and his family. From the safety of his villa in Mexico, this drug lord informed the chief that he was the one responsible for his family's murder. The chief, and some of his long-time friends in the tactical unit, decided to take care of these criminals themselves. Without any legal authority, the tactical unit went into Mexico and hunted down this drug lord. They didn't stop until they had killed him and his entire cartel!

I ask you, President Obama, "What right did the chief and his men have to do this?" Absolutely none! They entered a sovereign nation without its permission and murdered some of its citizens. It doesn't matter what kind of evil men they have killed! The men who actually committed these crimes were already dead! They were blown up along with the chief's family. Do you really believe that God and the Lord would want them to hunt down this drug cartel and kill them? Do you think the Lord wants any man to weed God's field especially for the reasons of men? Absolutely not! These men consciously chose to ignore God's word and the Lord's direction. Just like Adam and Eve, they did exactly what they wanted to. Now, they have become what they have killed! By doing so, they have chosen the path to destruction! The road to hell is paved with good intentions.

Just as God had instructed Nathan to give to King David his message, Jesus has instructed me to give you his message! This is you, President Obama! You and President Bush have sinned greatly against the Lord! There is no difference between this incident and what happened in the 9/11 attacks. The only difference between the two is the number of victims who died as a result of 9/11. To be a real Christian you must lay down your life, and you must give up your own way of thinking. But you have chosen not to do this! Jesus made it very clear that we are not to weed God's field! He instructed us to wait on God's harvest workers, but you have chosen not to listen to him! Instead, by your own admission, you have premeditatedly decided to eradicate your enemies!

Mr. President, you have chosen to follow your predecessor down the wide path he has cut through these evil weeds. You have foolishly let your council mislead you in their attempt to rid the world of evil doers. You have ordered your men to pull up these evil weeds! Your men are not angels, and you are not God! They are just seals obeying your commands, and you are just a misguided leader. Vengeance is when you choose to hunt down murderers and kill them outside the law. God made it very clear when he told us, *Vengeance is mine!* There are no laws under God which give you this right, and you know this! God's kingdom is not of this world, but the United States of America is. You have made the decision to give your nation what they want instead of listening to the Lord. Who are you presidents to defy the word of our God, and the Lord? You have chosen to serve your nation instead of the kingdom of heaven! You cannot live by the fruit of both trees! If you do, like Adam and Eve you will surely die (see Genesis 3:6-24)!

By your own admission you ordered your men to kill Bin Laden! It sounds like they killed him intentionally after the firefight was over! In your own words you said, "There was a firefight and then they killed Osama Bin Laden." Was this your directive? Did you order them to take no prisoners and make no arrests? I have no doubt that your men could have easily captured Bin Laden and taken him alive to stand trial, but instead they carried out your orders! After all, according to you, your Navy Seals are the best in the world at what they do. It's too bad you have chosen the wide gate to destruction like President Bush did. Well, what's done is done!

Then your men confiscated Bin Laden's body. Why did they take his body? They could have easily taken a DNA sample at the scene and left his body. Did you order your men to cut his head off and bring it back to you like President Bush did? It's now common knowledge that Bush's men took the wrong head! Was Bin Laden's head the DNA sample taken by your men? Did you order this, so that you could match his teeth to his dental records? Why did your men dump his body in the ocean? Was it to dispose of the evidence? How can you be tried for your crimes when there is no evidence? It sure wasn't done to give him a proper Muslim burial within twenty-four hours of his death! Are these the real reasons why you refuse to show the public the pictures of this assassination you ordered?

Your staff obviously goes to great lengths to be very careful about what they write for your speeches and what they release to the press. They're experts in the use of semantics which enables them to paint the picture you need them to. After all, your propaganda has to justify your actions, because the law sure doesn't! But no matter how tactful they are the truth always has a way of bleeding through. Holding back the facts to misrepresent the truth is the same as lying! All that is hidden will be known, Mr. President!

You have chosen to give the American people what they want instead of listening to God and the Lord. Now they have their pound of flesh! It's a sad State of the Union to see the American people celebrating the murder of another human being in the streets. It doesn't matter how evil and lost he was! It's still dead wrong! You cannot fight evil with evil! The American people are behaving like a mob of vigilantes at a lynching. It's really disheartening to see how blind and ignorant they are!

Their behavior is no better than the Arabs who have burned American flags and effigies of Bush in the streets! America claims to be a Christian nation founded on the principles of God, but it doesn't conduct itself like one! America's official motto is, "In God We Trust." But the reality is the American people have put their trust in you, Mr. President. Truthfully, you have let them down by giving them what they want. I highly doubt that God is going to bless America after witnessing the American people gloating in the streets at the murder of another human being!

You cannot fight the darkness of this world with darkness. It just spreads more evil! If you choose this path you only become what you are fighting! You must fight the darkness with light. The Italian mafia have a saying that is very true. When you think you're doing somebody, you're really doing yourself! You should know that you cannot fight fire with fire, but still you have chosen to do it! Light is the wisdom of the Lord and it is also the water of life. He gives it to us when we are thirsty, so that we can use it to extinguish the fires of the evil in this world! If you live by the sword then you will die by the sword! You will be judged by the same measure you have judged! It is by this sword that you will meet your fate!

It's easy to say, "God bless America," and "Justice has been done," when really all you have done is exact revenge for the American people. Talk is cheap! Why do you think so many have questioned what you have done? It's simple, they too can see the evil acts you have committed! You are only fooling the blind and ignorant of this world! I know, because I used to be one of them. Jesus said, *"Not everyone who says to me, 'Lord, Lord' will enter the kingdom of heaven, but only he who does the will of my Father who is in heaven"* (Matthew 7:21).

Mr. President, how can you claim to be a Christian when you have ordered the killing of another human being? You hypocrite! You are an insult to every real Christian who's ever tried to walk the walk! This is why I am compelled to address you directly, about your vile self-righteous hypocrisy! After all, I almost lost my soul because of the unchallenged influence evil people like you have over this world! I never realized just how brainwashed I was by the secular lies of you so-called Christian leaders. I couldn't see how dead people like you were until Jesus opened my eyes. You are just wolves in sheep's clothing. Your public admission of your conduct has proven you to be nothing more than a true Antichrist! I pray that you will wake up! Turn to the Lord for forgiveness, and repent for your evil sins before it's too late!

I don't for one minute condone what happened on 9/11. I'm fully aware of how sick and evil Osama Bin Laden was! By his own admission he has proven to the world that he was one of the most evil men of our time. But we must be greater than the evil men of this world! We cannot let them bring us down to their level! I definitely know how the families of the victims of 9/11 feel. After I lost my closest brother to murder, all I wanted was my pound of flesh! But 9/11 doesn't justify the criminal acts you have committed in the name of justice!

Man, can't you see your bigotry? You have become the evil you've killed! You can't keep doing whatever you want, to whomever you want, whenever you want! It doesn't make it right just because you claim to do it in the name of justice, freedom or democracy. Your double standard policy of do what I say and not what I do isn't cutting it with the world any longer! You are creating these terrorists by what you are doing! Every time you take one of these evil weeds out ten more will pop up in their place. It's like trying to shovel sand at the bottom of a dune. Haven't you learned anything from President Reagan's so-called war on drugs? Every time you take a dealer off the streets ten more appear on the corner to take their place. The American government's hypocritical domestic and foreign policies have engendered the Bin Ladens of this world! You don't have to look any further than America's own back yard for the proof! Don't you remember... Timothy McVeigh? Just wake up, and stop it!

Mr. President, you are the pot calling the kettle black! No pun intended. Your actions have proven this to be true! Bin Laden claimed to be a practicing Muslim. He claimed to be fighting the evil hypocrites of this world in support of the Muslim nations. His enemies were the evil and powerful men of the United States of America and their allies, who do whatever they want to the weak and innocent nations of the world! He managed to convince some lost souls that he was fighting a holy jihad in the name of Allah. Even though he had misled them, they were killing all kinds of innocent people while fighting for his cause! Bin Laden had absolutely no idea how to treat his fellow man, or live a righteous life before God.

You, sir, are no better! You claim to be a practising Christian. You, President Bush, and your government have misled the western nations into believing that you are fighting these evil terrorists in the name of justice. While actually in fact, you and your gang of nations are committing all kinds of injustices in the world while enforcing your real agenda! Meanwhile, you have managed to convince your men to kill all kinds of innocent people as they execute what you are really doing! You Christian hypocrites! You can't serve God and death! President Bush is responsible for the deaths of hundreds of thousands of people, and not just evil men like Bin Laden and his gang! Both of you are responsible for the deaths of many innocent people! God doesn't want either of you killing people, innocent or guilty! It doesn't matter what kind of picture you try to paint for the world to justify your actions. All you have done is fool a nation that is full of revenge-driven fools. But, the truth is the truth, Mr. President! By your actions you have become the beast you have slain! Amen.

You have entered a third country now without its permission! You ordered your men to attack a building and kill your enemies! Then, like Bin Laden, you took credit for you men's attack on the building and the murder of your enemies. Isn't that exactly what you claim Bin Laden did? Can't you see you are one and the same? It doesn't matter if it's for different reasons! Clearly you have made a grave misjudgment. You shouldn't have eaten this fruit! You are just opposing fingers of the same dark hand. Bin Laden was the middle finger to America and you are the thumbs up for America! Don't you see? All you have done by killing Bin Laden is prove to the world that you really are what he claimed you presidents to be all along! Vengeance is a vessel that doesn't hold water. I'm sure you'll realize this now that you've gotten your feet wet! No pun intended.

You might have gotten away with it in the here and now, but you will be accountable before the Lord! God knows exactly what's in the hearts and minds of men. I tell you this, the Lord hates hypocrites more than anything! Its not too late,

Mr. President, to wake up and turn to the Lord! You can still seek his forgiveness for what you have done! If you really are blind and ignorant then change your ways and seek his wisdom! But if in fact you are a wolf in sheep's clothing, then do what you must do! I pray for you, man.

The leaders of this world will be held far more accountable for their actions than their men will be! They are the evil guides of the wide road to perdition. Jesus said, *"Watch out for the false prophets! They dress up like sheep, but inside they are wolves who have come to attack you. You can tell what they are by what they do... You can tell the false prophets by their deeds"* (Matthew 7:15-16, 20, CEV). You have been served! You no longer have an excuse, now that you have seen yourself in the Lord's mirror! I have done my duty before God! You have been given the Lord's message! Amen.

If the leaders of this world would only follow the direction of their religions, and practice what they preach, we would have world peace. It's not rocket science! All they have to do is walk the walk. Christians, love your enemies and turn the other cheek. Don't hunt them down with vengeance and kill them. Vengeance is up to God, not man! Muslims, practice what it says in the Koran. If your enemy stops attacking you, then you must stop fighting back and live in peace. If each side stopped being hypocrites, we would have world peace. God blesses the peacemakers. Do not confuse them with the peacekeepers! They are not one and the same at all. We are to change this world through example, not with enforcement or fighting! Why can a man like Gandhi, who was not raised as a Christian, understand this message clearly when he studied the Bible as an adult, but the so-called Christian leaders of this world don't get it? It's because he received this light with an empty cup!

To truly change your ways in this world, three things are required. First, you must control your physical actions, and this is the easiest to do. Second, you must control what comes out of your mouth, because you will be judged by every word you say in this life. Third, you must change your mind, and this is the hardest thing to do. You must change your thoughts and your way of thinking. You must be like the Lord in your way of thinking, and you must not return to your old way of thinking.

This is very hard to do, and it takes a lot of effort. It will definitely not happen overnight. I know, because I have been trying to do this for years. We are not perfect, but we must continually keep trying. The devil will keep trying to make you return to your old ways. It says in the Bible, *"Dogs return to eat their vomit, just as fools repeat their foolishness"* (Proverbs 26:11, CEV). In other words, do not return to your old way of thinking. That's what Satan wants, because that's what he did. Lucifer fell from Yahweh's grace because he did not acknowledge Jesus as the Son of Man. The devil thought he was greater than Jesus because he was the angel of light and Jesus was just a lowly human to him.

It's a long, hard road, and you will fall down. Just keep getting up and continuing down the narrow path. Never give up! The Lord is always pulling on your string. In this world, do not try to change people on a personal level unless they approach you. It will just turn them off of the truth, unless they are ready and seeking it. Just worry about yourself, because this will be hard enough for you to do. Be an example for others. They will notice it in their own time and want to change, too! When they become curious and approach you, this is when you feed them.

Always try to be a good example for everyone. Always help anyone in need. This is what the Lord wants you to do. Remember, none of us are perfect. Just live one day at a time, because there may not even be a tomorrow. We all must just keep trying to refine our characters for the rest of our days. I love you all, especially the lost and blind. I pray that you will understand this message, wake up, and follow us home on the narrow path. Amen.

## Chapter 20

# Who Decides?

One thing in this world that will never change is what happens when you state your opinion to others. As soon as you voice your opinion, you have made a friend or an enemy. I have never been afraid of stating my opinion to others. Whether I was right or wrong in the mind of others has never mattered to me. I have always tried to be true to myself. I have not lived my life worrying about what other people think of me. I have always been man enough to admit my mistakes, and hopefully I learn from them. When I was younger, I had a lot of steadfast convictions. When I was twenty years old, I remember my Uncle Luigi telling me that I wouldn't always think the way I did. I told him, "You want to bet? I know what I know." Man, was I wrong!

Have you ever thought about free will? It's a very interesting concept. Is it real, an illusion, or an ingenious combination of both? Who decides our destiny, God or us? People of this world who do not believe in God usually believe that they are in total control of their lives. For instance, the comedian Bill Maher states in the movie *Religulous* that he is in total control of his life. He accepts total responsibility for all his decisions. This is what I call the super-mind concept. This fallacy is what happens when you allow your superhuman ego to control your life, and this is exactly what Satan wants. Bill is an atheist, someone who doesn't believe in God or the devil. Even the evil men of this world who do not follow God know that he exists. Like Satan, they just freely choose to go their own way. Maybe they're just weeds, and that's their destiny.

The concept of free will comes from the book of Genesis. I'm sure the atheists have never even considered this. The first example of free will can be traced back to Eve, when she decided to do what she wanted and listened to that snake instead of God. I personally believe that she was meant to do this, though, because if she didn't do it mankind would not be playing out this spiritual war of creation between God and Satan's gang. Think about it!

If we apply the principles of our memory to the future instead of the past, what happens? Our memory works like this. We can see and visualize everything that has happened to us in our lives, but we cannot change it. Apply this principle to our future. We can see everything that is going to happen to us, but we can't change it. What would be the point of living our lives if we already knew exactly what was going to happen? This is the reason we cannot see our futures. This creates in us our natural-born desire to experience what is going to happen next in our lives. None of us know if there will even be a tomorrow, or if the sun will come up. It could supernova while we are asleep and destroy our solar system, or we could just die in our sleep for some unknown reason. No. The future really happens according to God's will. What will be will be according to his design and what he allows.

This explains how Jesus and the prophets could see into the future. Jesus knew this and it was very evident in what he'd said to Peter during the their last supper. He told Peter, *"I promise you that before the rooster crows tonight you will say three times that you don't know me."* Peter strongly denied that he would ever forsake his master, but he did exactly that. Peter replied to Jesus, "Even if I have to die with you, I will never say that I don't know you"(Matthew 26:34–35, CEV). Peter thought that he knew himself, but despite his adamant convictions of loyalty to Jesus he still denied knowing him three times. You see, we do what we are meant to do in this life when we are tested, and not what we think we will. This is how we become who we really are and not who we think we are. There is only one way Jesus could have possibly known exactly what Peter was going to do. Peter's future must have already been known, and Jesus must of been able to see into it! Jesus did this on more than one occasion in his life. He knew exactly what Judas was going to do as well.

This also explains *déjà vu* experiences. I believe that a *déjà vu* experience happens when there is a connection between the master plan and the here and now. It's like a short circuit in their parallelism. The reality we experience in our lives is not controlled just by chance, coincidence or the decisions we think we make. There is definitely a divine synchronicity at work. We are not just biological compositions of matter, or just a bunch of beings made up of water and carbon-based materials by chance.

Don't be fooled by this school of thought! We really do matter! No pun intended. The universe has an order which is far too intricate on every level not to have been created by God. Believe me! Our destinies really are controlled by the will of God! When God wants the world to know something, he picks a man and delivers the information through him — whether it be a vision of future events or just scientific knowledge. People of the secular world just love to take the credit for discovering or inventing something. It feeds their superhuman ego, and the attention they desire.

It is written in the Bible that you cannot enter the kingdom of heaven unless your name is in the Book of the Lamb. It also says that the Book of the Lamb existed before the heavens and the earth. In other words, before God created the universe. God tells us that he knew us even before we were born, and that he knows exactly how many hairs we have on our heads. Do you? How could you? God created every one of us right down to our last thoughts, and these thoughts control every action we make in our lives. Have you ever asked yourself, *Why did I do that? I know better.* It's because you were meant to do it. Did you pick your brain out before you were born? Did you decide how you wanted it to work? Did you decide if you were going to be a genius like Einstein, a prophet like Moses, mentally handicapped, or a complete vegetable? Of course you didn't! God decided all things before the universe was even created. How do you think dogs know how to swim right from birth without being taught? Because God hardwired their brains. It's called innate intelligence. Are you not greater than a dog? Just think about how complex the human mind really is. It's definitely not the product of a random event! Think about how many hundreds of millions of sperm you beat in the great race to make it here. No. Believe me, it was planned that you'd be the one!

Don't get me wrong. We all do things in our own way. Some of us are very lazy, and some of us are real achievers. Some of us waste our lives, and some of us live very productive lives. Some of us do whatever we want in this life, and some of us live to serve others. We all do these things, and we all seem to make our own decisions, but is this really of our own free will? What I am saying is that we did not create ourselves. God created all of us, right down to what or who we choose to believe in! Do we really choose what we believe for ourselves, or has it been chosen for us by who we believe in? We did not hardwire our brains or program them; God did! We are what he wants us to be — good or bad, whether we want to accept this fact or not. He lets the rain fall on the good and bad alike, and he allows both to exist for now.

I have always thought I was in control of my life... until my brother was murdered. From then on, I was consumed with hate. All I wanted was vengeance. I just wanted to take out these people who had murdered my brother. For years, this was my life. Do you think this was how I wanted to live? Do you think I consciously picked this life for myself? Of course I didn't! It was my fate, and God's destiny for me! God let the devil do this to me, but I didn't know it at the time. I wouldn't be the man I am today, though, if I hadn't lived through these trials. This is what is referred to as the refiner's fire in the Bible. It will either consume you and burn you up, or it will refine you as pure as gold. God chose not to let me crash and burn in this life while I was being tested by Satan. He had a greater plan for me.

I don't exactly know why God chooses the people that he does, but he has his reasons. God is all-knowing, and omnipotent! I am not. When Moses was raised as Pharaoh's son, he had no idea how God planned to use him. All I know is what God has given me. In my heart, I was a natural-born warrior, like Peter. I've never worried about what other people think, and I've always been a straight shooter. Everyone who has met me knows right where I'm coming from.

I've always believed that it's important to live by some kind of code of ethics. Sometimes this way of thinking has created challenges for me, but that's okay; I've always been up for a good challenge. I was born a Leo, a natural born leader with the heart of a lion. I've never done anything halfway. It's all-or-nothing with me. I don't believe in sitting on the fence. God chose me for these qualities which he has instilled in me. He tempered me in the refiner's fire. All of my character traits, and all of the things I've had to endure, have prepared me for his mission.

Jesus has commissioned me to bring light into this world, and he has made me his lamp. I definitely did not pick this life. God has picked me, and he has prepared me to do his work. I often feel that I am not worthy to do this, but this is just a tool of the devil. Satan keeps on trying to bring us down psychologically, so we will not succeed. I have done many things in my life which I am very ashamed of, but in order to accept God's forgiveness we must first forgive ourselves. Once we have done this, we can get on with serving his greater purpose. There is nothing like the healing power of God's amazing grace. I have dragged my cross around in this life way too long. Now is the time for me to raise it above my head and show it to the world.

This is my cross, which I have been given in this life, and I am honoured to carry it for the Lord! (See Matthew 16:24-25.)

One of the wisest things I have ever heard was spoken by a man of peace. He claimed to be a Christian, a Buddhist, a Muslim, and a Jew. He said, "An eye for an eye will blind mankind!" He was a true man of God, and his name was Gandhi.

Vengeance will definitely blind the world. If you kill one person out of anger, it is like killing the whole world out of anger. If wars would never start, our lives would never be torn apart. We must live in peace, so live and let live. Love one another, including your enemies. War is just humanity sinking to its lowest level! We must ensure the preservation of peace. The only way we can accomplish this is through the personal abolishment of violence and war! I warn you, though! This is no easy task, and it will take all the courage you have to face the evil in this world. So, be brave! If you are wise, you will lay down your life for your brother, Jesus. The Lord commands us to do this. If a man does not live his life for something worth dying for, he is already dead! The truth is the only path to take in this life... so just live it! Stay gold, care deeply, and love one another. Peace.

On her deathbed, my grandmother told me a very wise thing. She said, "Do what you want to do in this life or you will only cheat yourself." Well, I personally want to lay down my life for my brother Jesus and serve my fellow man as he has commanded us to do. Amen.

# Chapter 21

# My Final Thoughts

One of the most important things you can do for yourself in life is read the Bible and study the parables! You must search for the wisdom and truth contained in them. For the last two thousand years, too many people have not realized that they are the fruit of the tree of life. Man was not meant to live on bread alone, but by the very word of God. I pray that God will enlighten you as he has me. The truth in the parables is timeless, and they contain every solution to life's problems. Pray the Lord's Prayer every day. It covers everything you could possibly need in this world. Live day by day to the fullest, because none of us know if there will even be a tomorrow.

I do not want this last chapter of my book to be an ending. Instead, I hope it will be a beginning for you. My desires and intentions are to help you adjust your focus in this world, so that you can live the rest of your life the way God wants you to.

I want to share with you the light which the Lord has given me, so that you, too, can find your way through the darkness of this world. I want many more of you to walk the same narrow path home as I do.

I do not want to be the last one on the path. We need to walk this walk together, so follow me home. I will not mislead you! If you are poor, don't worry. I have more than enough gold for all of you. My brother has given me enough to share with all of you for eternity. So take more than you need for yourselves and give it out to those who are poor as we once were. Do not keep it for yourselves, though (see Matthew 25:14–30)!

It might seem strange to hear that I'm not a very religious man. I do not have much faith in manmade religions. From what I have seen, they serve to separate men when they should bring them together. I feel very fortunate to have a direct connection with God. He has always been in me, for as long as I can remember. It's a one-on-one relationship, like Noah had. There were no manmade religions in Noah's day. Noah didn't just believe in God and have faith in him; Noah knew God, and God spoke directly to him.

Faith is a good thing, but I am not a man of faith. In the dictionary, faith is described as a firm belief in something for which there is no proof. I really feel for the people who have to cling to their faith and can only believe in God. Your Creator is not just a myth like Santa, or the Easter bunny. God is not something you grow out of, but rather someone who you must grow into. I am very fortunate to know God, and have him living in me. I am blessed that he has picked me. Christ said to his disciple, *"Thomas, do you have faith because you have seen me? The people who have faith in me without seeing me are the ones who are really bless-*

*ed!"* (John 20:29, CEV). So, keep your faith if this is all you have
been given. I tell you, as God's living witness, that he is real. He
loves you very much and he will always be there for you. When
you hear him knocking at the door to your heart, mind and soul;
let him in and he will never leave you (see Revelation 3:20-21). If
he's tugging at your string, let him reel you in.

Since the beginning of mankind, many men have communi-
cated with God in different ways. God spoke directly to Adam,
Noah and Abraham. God's angels spoke with Lot and Mary in
person. God appeared to Moses in the form of a burning bush.
The apostles walked with his Son in the flesh, and some of them,
like Thomas, still doubted. God speaks to me directly, so I do
not need faith. He doesn't talk to me in any of the forms which
I have previously described. God just comes right into my mind
and he gives me the knowledge that he wants me to have. This
is how he speaks to me directly. He is actually in me, and he
always has been. I know he is always there, because his light
comes right into my mind and then I can finally see. I hope you
too can experience what I am saying one day.

I started to write this book about six years ago, but for many
reasons I was never able to get around to finishing it. I wasn't
able to write a word for almost three years. I usually work fifteen-
hour days, five or six days a week. My job is very demanding,
and I had just been too tired to finish writing the book. That's
no excuse, though. God in his wisdom has made time for me to
finish it. He already knows what we need in this life. Be careful
what you ask for in this life, because you just might get it!

My mother was diagnosed with colon cancer ten years ago.
The cancer was quite advanced when her symptoms showed
up. She had to have major surgery, chemo therapy and radiation

treatments. She has beaten it, though, and is now almost eleven years cancer-free thanks to God. While she was going through this ordeal, I asked God if I could drink this cup for her instead. She has been through so much stress in her life, with her son being murdered, and her husband dying in a quad accident. I believe that she contracted the cancer from all the stress she has endured. In other words, the devil gave it to her as a test. Then my brother Mick was diagnosed with lymphatic cancer almost four years ago. I again asked God, "Let me drink this cup for him," because he has two children who still needed him around. Mick beat his cancer, too, thanks to God. He has since returned to work.

In September 2009, I was diagnosed with colon cancer. I received what I asked for, and I have absolutely no issues with it. I have not once experienced any anxiety, stress, or worry since being diagnosed. Both my mother and brother have been healed thanks to God. I have good doctors who have been screening me every two years. When they found the cancer, fortunately it was detected very early. I came home after receiving this news and talked with God. I told God, "I have no problem with you bringing me home early if you need me there. I have made my peace with you long ago. I've tried to live the way you want me to, but if you don't need me yet I would like to hang out here for a while because there are some things which I still want to do." I further expressed to him that I really didn't want to go through any major sickness or treatments like my mother had. I would rather just die quickly and come home.

To me, death is not an end. It's actually a beginning in heaven. I said to God, "Let me know tonight in a dream, or innately, what's going to happen with me." When I woke up in the morning at 4:30 to get ready for work, a quote from Bruce Lee came into my mind. I remember Bruce saying, "The fight is won before the physical contact even begins." I knew immediately that I was already cured! God had just given me my answer. I met with my pastor and told him everything. I said to him, "You can witness this. I have received this message from God, and I am already cured."

I underwent major surgery about three weeks later, and I had two feet of my transverse colon removed. The pathology report came back clean, and I was completely cured with just the surgery. Thanks to God, I didn't need any chemo therapy or radiation treatments. The good doctors are his instruments, but he is definitely the higher authority at work here. The type of cancer I had is the number two killer of people in North America. Five percent of all people who get it die no matter what they do. I was laid up for twelve weeks recovering, and this gave me the time to give my full attention to writing this book. When you go through something like this, you reset your life around what's most important. It's definitely a focus adjustment.

I knew immediately that God gave me this time to work on my book. There was nothing more pressing in my life than to finish writing it. In the forefront of my mind, I knew that if I didn't get serious and finish writing this book the Lord would take back what he has given me! Then I'd have nothing (see Luke 19:11-27). My greatest fear is knowing that I didn't put the light he gave me on the lampstand, for everyone to use to see their way through the darkness of this world! Thank you, God, for allowing me this time to do what Jesus has commanded me to do. I am truly blessed. Writing this book has allowed me to share the light my brother Jesus has given me with the world.

How bright it shines, and how far its light reaches through the darkness of this evil world, I leave in your hands my Father. Amen.

If I had spoken the truth contained in this book six hundred years ago, I would've been labelled a heretic and burned at the stake by the Catholics for challenging their hypocrisy. Today, I have no doubt that I could end up in the trunk of a car with a bullet in my head, for exposing the secular evil of the real powers that control this world! This does not concern me, though, because I am his living witness! The evil men of this world can only harm my body, and only if God allows it! They can never touch my soul! Amen (see Revelation 11:4-5).

I still go to church, but I am not a member! I now carry my cross above my head for my brothers, instead of dragging it around. I attend church so that the congregation can draw strength from me. When I am there, I also receive the Lord's energy. It's like I get my batteries recharged each week. I literally feel him in me. It's like when you open the door on a cold winter's day and you feel the shivers throughout your body. Except the feeling is not cold; it's warm and nice. It runs completely through me, right up to my brain. I know that I'm not the only one who feels him inside. I have friends who I have shared this experience with, and they too have felt the same thing. There is nothing quite like having God live inside you! Believe me, he is real, and I am his living witness!

Years ago, I considered going to college and studying to become a pastor, but I realized that God didn't want me to. He had already educated me in the refiner's fire. No Bible college in this world could teach me what he had already taught me. Jesus isn't interested in where I've gone to school. He only cares about what I have done with the wisdom I've been given. I have started speaking publicly in churches, and I hope to do many lectures and seminars for the rest of my days.

Thank you my brother, for saving my soul—I have listened to you! Your words of wisdom have humbled me... I will not weed our Father's field. But, I will feed the hungry with your fruit, share your gold with the poor, and shout what you have whispered to me from the housetops! Thank you for allowing me to take up my cross, and follow you home on the narrow path. I love you with all my heart, all my mind, and all my soul.

My hope is that after reading this book you will be changed forever too! I have absolutely no intentions to judge, condemn, insult, or offend anyone. My only desire is to pass on to you the truth my brother Jesus has shown me. I hope to give you a new set of eyes to see the world clearly in a new light as I have. I want to help the victims of the violence of this world make the right choices! Please lay down your desire for vengeance, and forgive the lost souls who have stolen life from you. I love you all, and may the good Lord bless you in this life, as he has me. Pray for the evil men of this world, so that they may change and turn to the Lord before it's too late for them. Thank you for restoring my dignity, my Father. Only you and I truly know how badly I lost it after my brother was murdered. My brother whispered to me, "Book 'em, Dano!" So I listened.

Amen.


A Story That Needs To Be Told!

# The End

This work was completed on Wednesday, May 25, 2011, in honour of my murdered brother's, Critter and Jesus.

# Epilogue

Dano is now in his fifties. During the first half of his life, he lived by a set of secular convictions he learned in this world. When he was thirty-six years old, his closest brother was murdered by some members of a criminal organization. These criminals have never been charged by the police. Because of these evil men, Dano was full of hate for years. He was obsessed with vengeance, and all he wanted was his pound of flesh.

God had different plans for Dano, though. He had no idea what lay ahead for him in this life. Dano discovered, after going through the various experiences in his life, that he was not the man he thought he was. Upon searching with all his heart, all his mind, and all his soul, the Lord enlightened him. God gave him the wisdom he was searching for, and Dano experienced his soul's awakening.

Dano was completely debased of his previous character, and his soul was stripped naked before the Lord. He had never experienced this type of humiliation before in his life. He instantly became a new man. Dano did not pick his life or the trials he endured. God allowed Satan to test him, and he was purified in the refiner's fire. He allowed Dano to be tempered through his life's experiences, so that he could use him for a greater purpose.

God has always been in Dano, and the good Lord has always been with him. Jesus instructed Dano to convey the light he was given to the world. This is why he has written this book. The secular hypocrisy of this world must be made visible, so that it does not continue to ruin so many lives. Too many people believe these lies, and they make crucial decisions in their lives based on them. Dano knows and understands the truth in the parables. The parables are the fruit of the tree of life, and the answer to every problem in life can be found in them.

The greatest secrets in this world are no longer secret, because man has had access to them for the last two thousand years. Jesus used the parables to adjust the focus of men in this world, and he was murdered for it. We must turn the other cheek and love our enemies. We must be greater than the evil men of this world. The greatest thing you can do in this world is lay down your life for your brother. Jesus did it for you! Now you can do it for him! Amen.